# EXPLORING UNIFICATION THEOLOGY

*Edited by*

**M. Darrol Bryant**
*and*
**Susan Hodges**

*Distributed by*
**The Rose of Sharon Press, Inc.**
**New York**

Conference Series, no. 1

# CONTENTS

# LIST OF PARTICIPANTS

## *Students from the Unification Theological Seminary, Barrytown, New York, U.S.A.*

| | |
|---|---|
| Janine Anderson | Guido Lombardi |
| Christa Dabeck | Lokesh Mazumdar |
| Adri De Groot | Linda Mitchell |
| Lloyd Eby | Diana Muxworthy |
| David Jarvis | Tom Selover |
| Mike Jenkins | Tirza Shilgi |
| Betsy Jones | Joe Stein |
| Farley Jones | Joe Stenson |
| Lynn Kim | Jonathan Wells |
| Klaus Lindner | |

## *Participants from Outside the Unification Movement.*

**Dr. M. Darrol Bryant**
Renison College
University of Waterloo
Waterloo, Ontario, Canada

**Dr. John Kuykendall**
Auburn University
Auburn, Alabama, U.S.A.

**Rev. Juris Calitis**
St. Andrews Evangelical
  Lutheran Latvian Church
Toronto, Ontario, Canada

**Dr. Herbert W. Richardson**
Institute of Christian Thought
St. Michael's College
Toronto, Ontario, Canada

**Dr. Elizabeth Clark**
Mary Washington College
Fredericksburg, Virginia, U.S.A.

**Dr. Rodney Sawatsky**
Conrad Grebel College
University of Waterloo
Waterloo, Ontario, Canada

**Dr. David Fee**
South Dakota State University
Brookings, South Dakota, U.S.A.

**Dr. Ward Wilson**
Viterbo College
LaCrosse, Wisconsin, U.S.A.

**Dr. Eugene Klaaren**
Wesleyan University
Middletown, Connecticut, U.S.A.

**Dr. Henry Vander Goot**
Calvin College
Grand Rapids, Michigan, U.S.A.

# INTRODUCTION

This volume grows out of a series of conversations at the Unification Theological Seminary in Barrytown, New York, during February and April of 1977. The participants in the conversations were students from the seminary and teachers of religious studies from colleges and universities in Canada and the United States. As should be obvious from the edited versions of our conversations, there was no design or agenda for these conversations other than that which arose from curiosity about the beliefs and practices of a group which has achieved a certain notoriety but little understanding over the last few years.

What is the Holy Spirit Association for the Unification of World Christianity? Who is Reverend Sun Myung Moon? What is this movement's relationship to the Christian tradition? What is the *Divine Principle?* How is the life of the movement organized? What do these people believe? These questions, large and unfocused, were all we brought with us. None of us, excepting Professor Herbert W. Richardson, had any prior familiarity with the Unification movement other than that available in the public media. Given that background, one perhaps shared by the reader, our interest was to hear the members of the Unification movement speak for themselves.

The result of these inauspicious beginnings is the present volume. Its aim is twofold. First, we want to share with other students of religion and interested members of the general public these conversations. It is our conviction that the primary obligation of the student of religion is to listen; these conversations allow us to hear members of the Unification movement articulate their beliefs. Once this primary obligation has been fulfilled we can then enter into critical conversation. This is the second aim of the volume: to initiate theological dialogue with the Unification movement. The structure of this volume reflects this twofold purpose.

Part I of the volume contains edited versions of conversations that ranged over the whole of Unification belief and practice. These five conversations have been edited from approximately six hundred pages of typescript. They have been edited in line with a single editorial principle: intelligibility. A tighter thematic arrangement of the material was considered, but it was decided to reproduce the conversations as they occurred, since they do follow certain topical lines. Although this procedure results in repetition, it also preserves the spontaneity of the original conversations. Moreover, much of the repetition is necessary since similar questions, for example, questions concerning the normative role of the *Divine Principle,* affect different aspects of Unification belief and practice in different ways.

The conversations are here reproduced under the headings of (I) Creation and Fall, (II) The Unification Movement and Christian Traditions, (III) The Millennial Landscape: Politics of the Kingdom, (IV) Practice, Style and Authority in the Unification Movement, and (V) the *Divine Principle:* Text and Principle. These headings are only a rough approximation of the material in each section. More than delimiting the precise content of each conversation, they tell the reader where to find the material of greatest interest to him. Taken together, these conversations constitute an introduction to the leading beliefs and concerns of the Unification movement. At the same time, the conversations disclose the considerable range of interpretation that exists within the movement itself.

To provide evidence of the wide range of interpretation one finds within the Unification movement on various points of doctrine and practice constitutes a chief merit of this document. Moreover, these conversations allow us to glimpse a movement *in the process of theological articulation and development.* These conversations then reveal a movement in the process of self-articulation, a process in which there is obviously room for a variety of readings. In part, this variety is a response to the variety of questions posed by those of us who came to these conversations from outside the Unification movement; but it is also clear that there is room within the Unification movement for significant differences.

Part II of the volume contains the papers written by Professors Vander Goot, Clark, Sawatsky and Bryant in response to our first meeting with members of the Unification Church and our initial readings of the *Divine Principle.* Those papers appear here as they were initially written, with the exception of the paper by Dr. Elizabeth Clark which she has substantially rewritten. These papers are followed by an edited version of the discussion that surrounded each paper.

The paper by Dr. Henry Vander Goot focuses on the doctrine of creation; the paper by Dr. Elizabeth Clark deals with women in Unification theology; Dr. Rodney Sawatsky's paper is directed toward sociological aspects of the Unification movement; and the paper by Dr. M. Darrol Bryant discusses Unification eschatology. The four papers included here do cover a significant range of theological questions. More importantly, the discussions that surround each paper are indicative of the Unification members' openness to hear and respond to substantive criticism.

A major editorial difficulty that arose from the transcripts of the meetings concerned the phrase "divine principle" and the shorthand expression "the principle." Sometimes this phrase was used to refer to the primary text of the movement, while at other times it was used to refer to the central principle or idea of the Unification movement. Moreover, there is disagreement within the Unification movement as to the meaning of the phrase "divine principle": whether or not that principle is primarily the "principle of creation" or the "principle of restoration" or both. Consequently, it was sometimes difficult to be sure of the referent or the meaning intended. Usually, however, the context was sufficiently clear to settle the issue. The editorial convention we have employed here is as follows. When the *Divine Principle* is capitalized and italicized, it refers to the primary text of the movement. (All of the references to this text are from the second edition of the *Divine Principle* published in New York by the Holy Spirit Association for the Unification of World Christianity in 1973. Throughout the conversations this text is often referred to as the "Black Book." This is in order to distinguish this edition from a 1950's edition known as the "Red Book." There is also a widespread expectation that there will be another edition of the *Divine Principle* in the future.) When the lower case is used (divine principle), it refers to the central idea or doctrine of the movement, a principle which is understood to underlie the whole cosmic process. When the form "the Principle" is used, it is short-hand for the "divine principle," although, as indicated, there is disagreement within the movement on this point. Except when the context indicates otherwise, the Principle can be understood to mean the principle of creation, that principle which underlies the cosmic process, or simply what the Unification members believe. Obviously, this is an issue which will require careful differentiation and clarification by the members of the Unification movement. Since that is a matter for the Unification movement itself to deal with, we have contented ourselves with the editorial device indicated above in order to minimize confusion.

The task of editing these materials has been difficult and instructive. The major difficulty is, of course, that of transposing the spoken word into intelligible written prose. This would have been an impossible task but for the cooperation of the participants. The students who participated in the meetings have read the edited versions of the conversations and have assented to what we have said they said. Similarly, the conversations have been circulated among the major participants from outside the Seminary and they too have graciously assented to the edited version of their words. We would like to thank Sarah Witt from the Seminary for undertaking the difficult task of transcribing our conversations, and Dean Stewart for arrangements that made our stay so pleasant.

It is hoped that the result of these efforts will be found useful and informative to a wider audience. Although we are aware of the controversy that surrounds the Unification movement, we have sought to avoid partisanship. It is clear, however, to those of us who had the opportunity to participate in these conversations that the Unification movement deserves a more sympathetic ear than it has generally received. We hope that this document will serve to place the whole discussion of the Unification movement on a different level, a level characterized by a willingness to allow the members of the movement to speak for themselves. Moreover, this document allows us to see a religious movement in the first stages of theological articulation in North America. Those of us who participated in these conversations found the emergent theologians of the Unification movement to be able young men and women who bring to the wider theological conversation the requisite virtues of passion, intelligence and commitment to the common enterprise of seeking the truth. This last reason alone warrants our placing this volume in the hands of a wider public.


## PREFACE TO THE SECOND EDITION

We are pleased with the reception which greeted publication of the first edition of *Exploring Unification Theology*. It appears that our hunch was correct: the conversations with the seminarians of the Unification Theological Seminary at Barrytown, New York — the heart of this volume — were of interest to a wider audience. It is hoped that this edition will assist in extending the circle of conversation and informed discussion. The appearance of this second edition has allowed us to make minor editorial corrections in the text; otherwise, the volume remains unaltered. We wish especially to thank John Maniatis for his assistance in this edition.


July 16, 1978                          Susan Hodges and Darrol Bryant

# PART I
# FIVE CONVERSATIONS

# CREATION AND FALL

*Dr. Darrol Bryant:* We don't have a structured agenda for this morning. However, I would suggest that we discuss the Unification movement under two headings: What is Unification as a sociological phenomenon? What is Unification as a theological posture? I have a lot of confidence that wherever we begin, everything will come out in the end. Why don't we just ask if there are particular questions that we would like to hear the young Unification theologians speak to.

*Dr. Rodney Sawatsky:* We had a conversation last night about the history of the movement and some aspects of Rev. Moon's story. I found it very interesting. Is everyone already familiar with that material?

*Dr. Eugene Klaaren:* It's certainly not familiar to me. In fact, I don't have the faintest idea at this point of what Rev. Moon has to do with you folks. I'm serious. I haven't heard his name mentioned. I saw his picture on the wall in the kitchen, but I don't understand what Rev. Moon means to you. I read the introduction to your *Divine Principle*. The introduction announces that the truth has arrived in the world and it has arrived through Rev. Moon. I'm exaggerating perhaps, but I really do not see how Rev. Moon relates to this movement. Does anybody want to enlighten me?

*Lynn Kim:* Okay. Rev. Moon was born in North Korea. His family converted to Christianity when he was about nine or ten. Before that they had been part of the basic Korean structure: Confucianism, Buddhism, Taoism. I understand that he himself had a very powerful conversion. I think it was connected with the healing of a child or something like that. Then he became well known for his participation in youth groups, prayer meetings, etc. He claims that when he was sixteen, he had a very powerful vision of Jesus on Easter morning. He then spent seven to nine years in intense spiritual search and study of the Scriptures. During part of this time he was studying electrical engineering in Japan. I met one of his close friends from that time who said that although he was studying electrical engineering, there were always three Bibles open in his room: one in English, one in Japanese and one in Korean. Each one was marked everywhere. At the end of that seven to nine years of search, and some teaching, he wrote the *Divine Principle.*

*Dr. Sawatsky:* Did he write that book?

*Lynn Kim:* No, not the Black Book version. During the first period of his ministry, Rev. Moon taught only orally. The first members heard the Principle in his sermons in which he was speaking about the Bible and interpreting sections of the Bible in relation to today. After teaching in North Korea from 1948 into 1950, he was imprisoned for about two and a half, almost three years. Then, during the Korean War, he was liberated; and it was in Pusan, as a refugee, that he first began writing a very brief, general version of the *Divine Principle.* *

*Dr. Sawatsky:* Then it seems to be the case that Moon's life precedes the *Divine Principle.* He influenced people through his oral teaching before he wrote anything down.

*Lynn Kim:* Yes, that's right.

*Dr. Bryant:* But I also get the impression that more is involved. Sometimes it sounds as if you're saying that the *Divine Principle* is "inspired." Yet I think I've heard a couple of people say that the Book doesn't matter; it's the Principle, not the Book that's important. You seem to think that in the writing of the *Divine Principle,* the Principle can be missed.

*Lloyd Eby:* I think that's true, actually.

*Dr. Henry Vander Goot:* Hold on! The whole point of the introduction to the *Divine Principle* is to let you know that this book contains the *Truth!* Wow! Now if it is the truth, it can't have missed the Principle. It can't be riddled by contradictions.

*Lloyd Eby:* We're much less bothered by this problem, I think, than the traditional book religions. One of the reasons we're less bothered by it is because of our understanding of the *Divine Principle* and our relationship to it. That understanding is medi-

*Editor's note:
  Subsequently the editors have heard variant accounts of the origins of the *Divine Principle.* We have never heard this particular story repeated; nor have we been able to confirm a version of the *Divine Principle* in Rev. Moon's own hand.

ated by Rev. Moon, and our relationship to Rev. Moon is extremely important. If you ask about the relationship of Rev. Moon to this movement, you'll get some kind of official answer. The more interesting question concerns the relationship of Rev. Moon to any particular member of this movement. I think you'll get as many different answers as there are members.

*Dr. Klaaren:* Is that really so?

*Lloyd Eby:* Our understanding of the Principle changes. I started out understanding the Principle as an external object. Then, gradually, with age and with deeper experiences with other people, with God, with Rev. Moon, and with the movement in general, I began to see the Principle as embodying the truth about many things. I would say that there are some problems in the matter of translation because the *Divine Principle* was written in Korean. Maybe words are mistranslated here and there. But that's not a serious problem. It's not a problem at all.

*Dr. Bryant:* I want to get back to your assertion that Rev. Moon means something different to each of you.

*Lloyd Eby:* I would say that our relationship with Rev. Moon varies with one's depth of understanding and with the length of time one has been in the movement. That's the best way of putting it.

*Dr. Bryant:* I'm not sure that that's very satisfactory. But you mentioned before that there's an official answer to the question "Who is Rev. Moon?" What would be the official answer?

*Lloyd Eby:* I think the official answer would be, and has been, that he is a prophet, a channel through whom God speaks.

*Dr. Vander Goot:* It seems to me that's a weak explanation. In the introduction to the *Divine Principle* it says that God in the fullness of time has sent His messenger to resolve the fundamental questions of life, and His messenger is Rev. Moon. The *Divine Principle* isn't just a systematic reflection on the meaning of faith; it claims to be a revelation from the Divine Being. So the sense in which Rev. Moon is a prophet or messenger is very special. Rev. Moon is not just a prophet in a general sense, but in the very specific sense that he announces and discloses the divine will.

*Dr. Bryant:* Isn't part of our problem our different understandings of the word "prophet?" Some say that Rev. Moon is a prophet as Moses is a Prophet: Moses reveals the Law. Others say no, it's not like that at all. Moon is a prophet as John the Baptist is a prophet in that both announce that "the time is at hand." Rev. Moon doesn't seem to be a prophet as Luther and Calvin are prophets; he's not a reformer. He's not a prophet like Amos: a

prophet who reminds people that they are straying away from the
Covenant. So I think of Moses and John the Baptist as analogies
for how you understand Rev. Moon. Would you people agree?

*Farley Jones:* I don't think so. I think that the reason we hesitate to explain the role of Rev. Moon is because it's somewhat
radical. We believe that he is coming in the role of the Third
Adam. We believe that God is about to initiate a new history, a
new creation, a restoration of the original ideal which was lost at
the time of Adam. Since then God's work in history has been the
reestablishment of the Adamic position, the position of Adam and
Eve as the True Parents of mankind. Our belief is that Jesus came
in that role, but as it says in the *Divine Principle,* because He was
rejected by the people of His age, He was not able to fulfill His
role completely. So we see Rev. Moon as chosen to fulfill that role.
However, we are also aware that Rev. Moon's success is somewhat
conditional. As in Jesus' case, Rev. Moon has to fulfill certain
conditions. Those around him have to support him so that he can
fulfill that role. We believe that through him, and through his efforts, God is working to establish a new family of mankind which
will be the fulfillment of God's original ideal. So, in that sense,
he's all the things that people have said he is. He is a prophet, he's
the founder of the Unification Church; but more than that, we see
him in the role of potential True Parent of mankind, and his wife,
the feminine side, as the True Mother of mankind.

*Dr. Bryant:* Now, that's the strongest statement I've heard
about Rev. Moon. I saw that written in the *Divine Principle,* but in
talking to several people about it in the last few days, I've never
heard anyone say as clearly as you have that Rev. Moon is potentially the Third Adam.

*Farley Jones:* People are reluctant to say it because it is such a
strong statement. It's shocking, and they're afraid it's going to be
alienating. And so they're hesitant. The reason I said it is because I
assumed that at some point you're all going to read the *Divine
Principle;* and if you're going to read it, you're going to find it out
anyway. (laughter)

*Lynn Kim:* Yes, I hesitated, but I'm grateful it's said because
otherwise you're going to be asking and we're going to be avoid-
ing. You were asking about it very clearly last night, but the mood
at our table was one of avoidance. I hesitated to break the kind of
sidestepping that was going on.

*Dr. Herbert Richardson:* Before we all start jumping around,
I want to say that I don't find that to be a very strong statement at
all. That is, it's very dramatic, but from one point of view it's a lit-

tle bit like somebody announcing that he's the first *"Ishkabibel."* (laughter) Everyone might be surprised, but first we have to know what that means. To put it in technical theological terms, I don't know any place in the Christian tradition where there's much invested, on a confessional level, in some particular conception of Adam. It's certainly not the case that "Second Adam" is an important title for Jesus. To some extent, the Unification Church is saying that Jesus was a Second Adam to clear the way for Moon to be a Third Adam, but I don't think that "Second Adam" Christology is important in the New Testament or in the teaching of the Church. Farley's statement may affect us emotionally, but theologically and logically, I don't see that it carries much weight.

*Dr. Vander Goot:* Well, maybe not specifically, but the concept to which the term refers is very important. I mean, there is *one* Redeemer figure in the history of Christian theology. There is a fundamental difference there between the theology of the Second Adam, which may not be important in Christian theology, and the idea of more than one Redeemer.

*Dr. Richardson:* Just this point, though. The formula "Redeemer figure" is a theological construction. It's not in Scripture, for example, and it's not in the classical theological tradition. It's what the theologian thinks up as a general category in order to assimilate a number of terms — Second Adam, Messiah, etc. But there's no necessity, it seems to me, that we do this. We might readily leave them separate for awhile and let them each have their own intrinsic development before we start comparing them. That's my point.

*Dr. Bryant:* I think you're anticipating that we'll jump all over Farley and anyone else for having said what he said. I don't think that's going to happen. I think that he gave a helpful clarification of the question so that we don't go around thinking that Moon is like John Calvin or like Amos or Mohammed or any other figure. This other category, Adam, which at this moment is just another category, may help us. But there is another way to learn about Rev. Moon. I keep hearing so much here about the experience of the family. I think there's an experiential content that's every bit as important as this theological articulation and argumentation. My impression is that it's absolutely crucial for us to see these two elements in relation to each other.

*Lloyd Eby:* I think what's sometimes interpreted by an outsider as avoidance is actually honesty. Before I ever came to the Church, I heard that Rev. Moon was supposed to be the Messiah. I thought that was nonsense. And when I first heard him speak, my honest impression was that he was simply a great preacher and a very courageous man. It so happened that he had to stand up to a very angry crowd that night. A few months later my relationship to him changed and he became my spiritual teacher, my guru. But I still didn't think of him as more than that, and I was willing to pursue that relationship for awhile. If someone had asked me at that time who Rev. Moon was, that's what I would have told them. A little later on, he became, in a sense, my employer, which sounds like a step down from guru, but is actually (laughter) a step up in the sense that it made my relationship with him more normal and more human. At the present time I would say that my relationship with him is still developing. He's becoming, for me, some kind of father: my adopted father. The motive that has led me through these transformations has been a desire to deepen my relationship with God. At each step of the way, the change in my relationship to Rev. Moon has been a reflection of that fundamental urge. So if you want an honest answer from me, I can't tell you that Rev. Moon is the Messiah; but maybe that'll turn out to be the case. It's certainly a possibility. I would say that I now see him as my adopted father.

*Dr. Elizabeth Clark:* It is my impression that the Unification Church says that one reason why Jesus did not fulfill whatever it was people thought he was going to fulfill is because he did not marry and have a family. Rev. Moon is now fulfilling that requirement, and preaching a new idea about the family. Would someone talk about that?

*Joe Stenson:* I think that in order to talk about the idea of the family and its relationship to Jesus as someone who also comes in the position of Adam, you have to talk about the creation of Adam and the original intention of God that was lost in the Fall. In answer to the question "Who is Rev. Moon?" anyone can say, "Well, he's the Messiah or he's this or he's that." But a complete answer must explain what we understand by that. I think in order to say that Rev. Moon is in the position of a True Parent, or in the position of True Adam, we must explain what that means. We must explain what the Creation means to us, who Adam and Eve are to us, what was lost at the Fall, what Jesus restored and failed to restore, and what Rev. Moon can do, or is in the position to do.

*Dr. Bryant:* Okay, then. Sketch the theological context.

*Joe Stenson:* Now this is my perception of the context of our belief. We believe the Adam and Eve story in Genesis. We understand it as the story of God's intention for mankind. God creates a male and a female. He creates the male part of mankind and the female part of mankind as equal and complementary. Adam and Eve, when they were created, were to grow and develop to become perfect children of God. Adam and Eve were not created perfect, but were created to grow to perfection. During the time of growth, Adam and Eve had free will. At some point during Adam and Eve's growth process, they were exposed to the influence of evil which is symbolized in the Genesis account by the serpent whom we interpret, and I think Christian theology interprets, as Satan. Through their relationship with Satan, with the serpent, the Fall of man occurs: a fall that has its roots in the misuse of love.

Genesis uses archetypes and symbols to tell the story. For example, Genesis says that they ate an apple. What does that mean? To us, it's a symbol of sexuality, of the misuse of sex. Satan, the serpent, seduces Eve and Eve succumbs. This is, in a sense, a spiritual Fall. Then Eve, realizing what has happened and realizing that her intended mate was not Satan, but Adam, seduces Adam. She wants to fulfill their intended relationship. However, Adam and Eve's sexual union constitutes, at that point, a misuse of love. Their love is centered on themselves rather than centered on God. It's not for the fulfillment of God's purpose. This, then, is the Fall of humankind. It's primarily a sexual Fall and a misuse of God's love, love which we would call "principled" love.

In order to restore principled love, we must get new parents. Our first parents, Adam and Eve, were claimed by Satan. The progeny of these parents, then, always have the potential of being claimed by Satan. Thus the history of mankind has been the multiplication of the progeny of Adam and Eve, a progeny claimed by Satan. In order for Adam's progeny to be restored to God, then, a figure must come who can reverse the whole process. A figure must come in the position of Adam to become the new parent of mankind. Jesus is in that position. When Jesus came as the new Adam, He was to fulfill certain conditions that were lost when Adam and Eve fell. However, because He wasn't accepted, but was rejected and killed, He didn't have the opportunity to completely fulfill His mission. So then the providence of God was extended and more of a foundation prepared in order for another figure to come in that position.

*Lynn Kim:* I think that was pretty thorough. There are a couple of things I would like to add concerning our concept of the immaturity of Adam and Eve, and our use of the term "perfection." The term "perfection" refers to a relationship with God. A perfect man is someone who loves God so much that his heart resonates with God's heart. A perfect man would feel what God feels for others. So in the beginning, then, God's desire was for a complete love relationship: a relationship so profound for Adam and Eve that it would have been impossible for them to separate from God. It was not impossible in terms of a philosophical notion of free will, but impossible because of the depth of the relationship. While they were growing in this relationship they were in a vulnerable position. This is why there was the commandment "Do not eat of the fruit." When you're not yet in a complete love relationship with God, it's possible for love to go in another direction, to become self-centered or directed to something other than God. I think we've all experienced this possibility in our own lives. So, then, that's how the Fall could happen. Man, through his freedom, a freedom given by God primarily because of the relationship He wants to have with man, falls.

*Dr. Sawatsky:* If you had a sexual Fall, do you have a sexual salvation?

*Lynn Kim:* That's another thing I want to discuss. The one thing that Joe said that I would not agree with and would want to clarify is the use of the word "sexual." We teach that the Fall comes about from a misuse of love. Adam and Eve were to become one with God in love, but the love became directed toward Satan, and became a self-centered love between them. Before Adam became a perfect man and one with God, and before Eve became a perfect woman and one with God, they united together. They did not as yet know God completely within their own lives, so when they united together, they were not able, in a sense, to give God to their children. God was not in them, so God could not be in their children. They could not give their children what they didn't have.

*Dr. Sawatsky:* Let's follow that through. Is all sexual activity of imperfect man fallen?

*Lynn Kim:* To us, sexuality is the vehicle through which original sin is passed on. The original sin is the separation from God on the level of love which is then multiplied through sexuality. It's not — how can I say it — that we hate sex. It's not that. It has a much deeper significance.

*Dr. Bryant:* But it's more than a symbol. It is indeed the way that sin is perpetuated in history, according to your beliefs.

*Diana Muxworthy:* I think it's important that within the principle of creation — for me the principle of creation is the essence of the *Divine Principle* — man fell, and that the whole point of history is to restore him. So it's essential that we understand that we are co-creators in restoration. The center of the *Divine Principle* is its understanding of why we were created, under what laws. I know it was most confusing to me when I first heard the *Divine Principle.* What does this mean to me when they speak of fulfilling God's purpose? What is my purpose? To know that I had to fully understand what was meant by fulfilling the Three Blessings.

The purpose of creation is the fulfillment of the Three Blessings, the Three Blessings as they are laid out in Genesis. In our understanding, the first blessing, the perfection of individuality, aims at oneness with God. You love as God loves, you think as God thinks. It is a very deep experience that we all taste at some time in our life, or can if we try. Then on that foundation of perfected individuality in tune with God comes the creation of the family, the second blessing, the multiplication and fruitfulness commanded in Genesis. When you have perfected your individuality so that your heart is one with God's heart and your mind is one with God's mind, and your mind and body are integrated, then you can create a family that is in tune with the perfection in you and in your mate. So these are the first two blessings. The third blessing is dominion over creation. In Genesis it says that because you are so connected with God's love your dominion over the creation or your use of all the natural resources is in tune with the love that God has for those resources. The Three Blessings have to be understood if one wants to understand the Unification idea of creation.

*Linda Mitchell:* When we refer to the Three Blessings we refer specifically, as Diana explained, to the Genesis account. The Three Blessings are more or less God's intention for mankind. In Genesis they are expressed in these words: "Be fruitful, multiply, and take dominion over the earth." As Diana was explaining before, we believe that these words represent God's intention.

*Dr. Bryant:* Can you say something about the implications of the Three Blessings for the family and the community? I take it, for example, that family relates to what we were talking about last night concerning spiritual mothers and fathers, and to the development of a parental heart as a spiritual discipline that would precede getting married and having children.

*Lynn Kim:* Right now, especially in America, we're in a transition period because of our long-term connection with the fallen history of humankind and because of the obvious imperfection in ourselves. We're desperately seeking to know God and to bring our bodies into harmony with our minds. So the Unification members are in a voluntary period of separation of husbands and wives in order to come to know God and bring about the unity of our bodies and our minds before we have children. This is the period we're in now in America. But the next step, which is very important to all of us, will be the marital relationship.

*Tom Selover:* It is important to understand what we mean by marriage. It is not the typical get-together that closes the couple off from everyone else.

*Joe Stenson:* Individual and family relationships are the way in which God works with us. That's the idea.

*Dr. Sawatsky:* To get back to what you were saying before, are you implying that until you feel that you have attained a certain level of perfection, a oneness with God, you will be celibate? Will the couples that are currently married abstain from sexual activity until a certain point?

*Lynn Kim:* Many do.

*Dr. Sawatsky:* It wouldn't be required? Would there be a period in which sexuality is set aside for a reason? A number of times I have asked about married couples and people seem a little hesitant about replying. What I'm catching is that the question is not particularly important here because few of you are married, and those who are don't have their mates here.

*Farley Jones:* I'm married.

*Dr. Sawatsky:* Your mate is living with you?

*Farley Jones:* Well, right now, she's travelling frequently to visit church centers. She's doing itinerary work on behalf of the Church. But basically, we're a married couple, a normal man and wife. We have two children. Now that doesn't mean my wife and I have achieved any kind of perfection. What it does mean is that before we were married in the Church, we demonstrated our faith for a period of time and were evaluated by superiors in the Church as having achieved sufficient spiritual maturity for marriage. So even though we teach that the ideal is for an individual man and an individual woman to achieve a state of maturity and oneness with God before marriage, we're also aware of the practical necessity to continue the human race. Because we are all from a fallen background, our ideals are going to be realized only progressively and not all at once.

*Dr. Bryant:* But when you say before marriage, don't you really mean before sexual intercourse? If, as Lynn said, you see the Fall as misdirected love, why must you see the Fall as specifically sexual? Why not use another category? For example, idolatry. Original sin is idolatry, not sexuality.

*Lynn Kim:* That's the interpretation of it — sin as sexuality — that I was afraid would come up when Joe was using the word "sexual." The term is misleading. We're saying original sin is the misuse of love. Call it idolatry; I don't care what you call it. Essentially, it's not loving God first.

*Dr. Richardson:* Just an observation. What you say is different from what Farley says and what Joe says, and I would very much like to hear what Farley would say on this point. He started to say something and you said, "Well, I was afraid such an interpretation would come up." One of the things that's most interesting to us is to hear Joe say something that is different from what you're saying and to hear Farley say something that is different from both. It's in hearing many different views that the reality and richness of the religious tradition is seen.

*Dr. Sawatsky:* Indeed. This is what is fascinating to hear: the range of interpretation within the Unification movement.

*Diana Muxworthy:* It's also interesting because Joe is not married, Lynn is married but without children, and Farley has children. Maybe they each have a different experience of the Principle.

I don't think that it's Unification teaching that people are supposed to become perfect in their relationship with God before they marry. I think marriage is part of the process of perfecting the relationship with God. Having children is also part of the process, since your children educate you too. If you have children and have trouble and yet you love them unconditionally, you can sympathize more with God. You can put yourself in God's position and understand how God relates to you.

*Dr. Sawatsky:* But there's still some kind of priority placed on personal development in this period of abstinence and preparation.

*Lynn Kim:* I didn't mean to keep pushing this because I don't think we are hung up on this sex thing. But sex and religion do go hand in hand. (laughter)

*Dr. Sawatsky:* Are there two levels of perfection? That is, would Lynn in the situation of living apart from her husband — not having children and not having intercourse — be in a more perfect state than somebody who is having children?

*Chorus of students:* Just the opposite!

*Linda Mitchell:* Here's the whole point of being separate. What has happened throughout history is that God has always received leftovers although God should be first and foremost in our lives. In order for us to be capable of loving another person, we must see that the love doesn't come from us, but actually, literally, comes from God. And so in order to be a channel of God's love, we learn to give to our brothers in an unmarried single state when we're seeking to know God. And then, when we feel that we're ready to begin loving our mate, we can get married. We will put God before our partner. Then we're able to grow to love our partner more and to grow to love God more. On the foundation of that love, you are free to have children because then you have a very substantial relationship not only with your mate, but also with God. On that foundation, you, as a couple, can really give God's love to your children to whatever degree you have God's love in you. This doesn't mean we're perfect. We only can give as much of God's love as we have of it.

*Dr. Klaaren:* Aren't you merely making a theological virtue out of the chronological and biological fact that you're unmarried before you marry, and married before you have children? (laughter)

*Dr. Vander Goot:* I think God established the natural order. And, in fact, the natural order reflects the theology. It isn't the other way around. That's built right into Unification theology in the internal-external stuff. Of course, that's the way it is in the external order because that's God's creation. Theologically you follow the same sequence that you follow spiritually.

*Lloyd Eby:* That's the sense of what we mean by perfection too. A lot of people tend to see perfection as something fixed and final, but we talk about perfection as a process. When I look at Farley, for example, I can think of him as perfect in the sense that he has achieved a certain relationship between his mind and his body that I admire and try to imitate. Farley has something that I want — not something I want to take from him, but that I want. It's not as if I think that every move he makes is going to be the absolute living end. (laughter) Perfection simply means that we have overcome enough so that we can really start to live and develop. It's like a new birth.

*Lokesh Mazumdar:* May I add two points? The *Divine Principle* says man is originally created with a potentially perfect mind and that as a result of the Fall, man has a fallen mind. So there's some kind of a wall there between the two dimensions of his mind. It is hoped that as a person gets closer to the comprehension of truth, the pieces sort of fall together. Something from outside contacts the fertile ground inside, somewhere deep inside that has never really exercised itself. So there's a kind of *re-creation* that takes place almost instantaneously. This doesn't always happen, but over the course of a lifetime and over the course of one's growth in the spirit world, it is hoped that this awareness increases. That accounts for the fact that sometimes a person says "I knew that," "I've heard all this before," "This sounds very familiar," "Now I can see where the pieces fit."

The other point involves my personal feelings about a confusion when you talk of love. Love is love. There's nothing evil about love. But when we refer to fallen love or satanic love, we mean a kind of love opposed to divine love. It is the lesser degree of love. Man never really experienced that greater love of God, and so he functions on one level and downward from that level. This is one reason why I would think that it's very difficult for people who have never experienced the good situation of God's love to go beyond their experience, and to say, "Well, now, let's see, there's something missing in my life — what could that be?"

*Dr. Bryant:* But you *do* talk about the Fall in terms of sexuality. You don't talk about fallenness in other terms.

*Lokesh Mazumdar:* I would talk about fallenness in many terms.

*Dr. Bryant:* There are other aspects of fallen love, too. It seems that what you have done is picked up this form of fallenness — the sexual — and stressed it in order to understand what fallenness is in general. That may have to do with the fact that the family is your key concept in the attempt to understand the order of creation. Therefore you understand fallenness in terms of distorted sexuality.

*Lloyd Eby:* I want to talk for a minute about sin. I think you need to distinguish between two things. I think that we see sin as a distortion of parentage. In other words, because of what Adam and Eve did, the human race has, as it were, the wrong parentage. The human race is designed to have God as its True Parent. But because of the Fall, Satan became the parent of the human race. So to say that someone is without sin means that he has God as his True Parent.

The second thing to talk about is man's sinful nature which comes as the result of the "original" sin. That sinful nature can be expressed in many, many ways. It can be expressed as hate and lust and all the other things that people talk about as sin, as manifestations of our sinful nature. But, at its most basic level, sexuality, apart from sexuality as an expression of being joined to the parentage of God, serves to perpetuate sinful parentage. Therefore, it's necessary to restore sexuality to God as a parent. And then, after that, it's necessary to solve also all the other expressions of sin. Thus you need to distinguish between sin as parentage and sin as an expression of sinful or fallen nature.

*Dr. Klaaren:* What's the sexual connection between God's creation and God?

*Lloyd Eby:* Sexuality is the way parentage is transmitted, right? So because Adam and Eve had the relationship with the archangel, the archangel became, as it were, the parent of the human race. Therefore, Jesus could say, for example, that "You are children of your father, the Devil." And he means that both metaphorically and literally. Therefore, in order to restore God as parent of the human race, it's necessary that a new Adam come from God, a person who is not sinful and is not the product of fallen parentage. Then, through his activity with his family, a new lineage of the human race can be established with him and, through him, with God as the True Parent of the human race. There's a sense in which the fallen Adam and Eve are still the children of God because God is their origin. There's also a sense in which they're not the children of God because Satan has usurped the position of their parent. Does that make sense?

*Dr. Klaaren:* I follow what you're saying.

*Janine Anderson:* The sex act is the mechanism through which original sin is passed on. So the whole point about restoring ourselves is to be able to love in a way that's centered on God. Then, when you have children, original sin is not passed on. The sex act is the physical mechanism for the continuation of original sin.

*Joe Stenson:* I think it's very true that our stress on sexuality comes from the fact that sexuality is the vehicle through which the whole thing started, according to the interpretation or the meaning that we give to the story in Genesis. Our particular interpretation, which isn't all that uncommon, would say that sexuality was the vehicle through which the Fall occurred and through which the Fall is multiplied.

*Lloyd Eby:* Eventually, we can talk about love and the love of God and the relationship with God. But if in restoration everything is going to be reversed, the reversal must involve the vehicle. Sexuality is going to be purified. Then the sex act and sexual intercourse will be in its proper perspective as part of the relationship with God.

*Dr. Richardson:* The thing that bothers me here is that this is exactly the kind of thing that is said that lets Ted Patrick say, when he's deprogramming somebody: "You say Rev. Moon is your True Father. That means he had sexual intercourse with your mother." If you talk to me about sexual intercourse as the way in which parentage comes into existence, then Ted Patrick can say that. Now surely you don't want to hold that view. I think what you want to say is something like this. If Rev. Moon can be your True Father, that means that parentage does not originate through sexual intercourse, but through a spiritual or right love relationship of which sexual intercourse may or may not be the right expression. So, for example, you would say that it's quite possible that someone might have a physical parent different from his true parent. I'm not necessarily talking of parentage in the religious sense. Take a child that is born from parents that don't want the child. They put the child up for adoption, and the adopted parents take the child and become the true parents of that child through their act of love. I think that's the view of parentage that you want to hold. In this view, rightly ordered sexual intercourse is the way in which grace is propagated by love, which controls everything, even sex.

*Dr. Sawatsky:* Let's check that. Is it the case now that a couple which has been perfected to some extent by their love of God has more perfect children? And if that is so, then are we picking up a notion that grace is transferred through correct parentage?

*Dr. Klaaren:* I have a suggestion here. Having been here and having heard you talk, I'm reminded of Calvin in his understanding of the Real Presence. Calvin argued with Luther that the Real Presence isn't in the wafer, but is in the whole liturgical act. To focus on perfection as transmitted through the act of intercourse itself is like focusing on Christ as present in the wafer. You can say that the real perfection is communicated in the wafer or in the whole liturgical act. Similarly, you can say that perfection is communicated in the act of intercourse or in the totality of family life and interaction. And then one could say — and surely this is our experience — that an act of sexual intercourse expresses the total ethos of the on-going living relation with the other person. And in that sense, one could argue that the child born of that relation carries with him the weight of the total relationship. But going against this suggestion, I feel that Unification theology in general is so Gestalt-oriented and process-oriented that you immediately run into trouble when you try to pick up any one belief and ask "How do you evaluate this?"

*Lokesh Mazumdar:* Joe used the term "principled love" for which you used the word "grace." Principled love is a pretty heavy term that was not explained completely. Therefore, it deteriorated into sexual love and sexuality.

*Dr. Sawatsky:* Of what import is Rev. Moon's perfection? And his passing this perfection on to his progeny? Is it separate from your perfection and your passing this on to your progeny?

Can the Third Adam miss, but those of you who are his spiritual children make it?

*Jonathan Wells:* He constantly tells us to be prepared for that eventuality. He's always challenging us on that point.

*Rev. Juris Calitis:* If he's crucified, or whatever?

*Jonathan Wells:* Or if he were to leave the Movement or be deprogrammed. (laughter)

*Dr. Richardson:* Let me tell you the most startling thing I've heard in all the time I've been here. I think it was from you, Tom, or it may have been from someone else. Part of the doctrine is that just as a father and mother want their children to become more than they are, so Rev. Moon seeks and anticipates that his children will become more than he is. He challenges them to be more than he is whether he is deprogrammed or not.

*Joe Stenson:* Yes. His family, and us, and all.

*Dr. Sawatsky:* Let's catch that parable then. If Rev. Moon could miss it and you can make it, why couldn't Jesus miss it and His followers make it?

*Lloyd Eby:* That's an interesting question. Once one sees that people are a composite of spirit and body, or physical and spiritual, one sees then that divine lineage has to be passed on both spiritually and physically. The divine lineage was disrupted through the Fall of man both spiritually and physically. Then, in order for the divine lineage to be restored, whoever initiates the restoration has to restore the divine lineage both spiritually and physically. Now, Unification theology claims that Jesus was successful in restoring the divine lineage spiritually, but because of various difficulties, He was not successful in restoring the divine lineage physically.

*Dr. Sawatsky:* You mean because He didn't get married?

*Lloyd Eby:* Well, yes, that's part of it. Now, if it's true that Rev. Moon occupies the same position and has the same mission as the Second Adam, and if it's true that he has, in fact, succeeded in restoring that divine lineage to his own family, and also has extended his family to people who weren't born of him physically and has thus restored them to this divine lineage, then if he could be deprogrammed now, the restoration would still continue.

*Dr. Sawatsky:* Would that depend upon his having physical children?

*Dr. Clark:* What part do his physical children play in all this?

*Rev. Calitis:* You seem to say that restoration is a physical result of Rev. Moon's position. But then you say that the restoration is passed on to others not physically related to him. We can understand how something is passed on through the genes. But you speak of some kind of grace that is transferred by another process to all those Rev. Moon marries and to their progeny as well. Transferred by a spiritual transfer, I suppose. Do you have two mechanisms operating here? One for physical transmission and another for spiritual transmission?

*Farley Jones:* We conceive of that transferral taking place through the blessing of marriage. At the time of the wedding ceremony, there's what we call the Holy Wine Ceremony which is more than symbolic. It represents or communicates something from Rev. Moon's spirituality to the couple.

*Dr. Sawatsky:* That's helpful because one of the differences between Rev. Moon and Jesus is that Jesus attended a marriage but, as far as we know, he didn't marry. And he wasn't the one to perform the marriage. He wasn't extending the family in that sense. The other part of the question is to what extent Moon's own progeny are important in the physical restoration. Your suggestion is that his spiritual progeny are all those people who are married by him. They can continue the restoration even if his own progeny or he himself are deprogrammed.

*Farley Jones:* My own sense is that you are speaking too strongly when you say that I or someone else who has been married by Rev. Moon could succeed him in what he's doing, in what he represents. Yet I do believe that there is something inherited from him spiritually, through the blessing of the marriage.

*Dr. Clark:* Does marriage have sacramental meaning?

*Lynn Kim:* The marriage ceremony itself is sacramental.

*Dr. Clark:* Can we unpack that term a little? What do you mean by sacramental? It has meant different things in the different Christian traditions. Is there any other act in the Unification Church that's considered a sacrament, something like the Lord's Supper, or something which has that status, which would be in the same category?

*Farley Jones:* I think that marriage is the only act that we would understand in that way right now.

*Joe Stenson:* I think there is something interesting about this wedding ceremony, although I've never been to one. This is all second-hand. (laughter) To my knowledge, it combines elements of several sacraments. For instance, Farley speaks of the Holy Wine Ceremony. Part of the ceremony also involves the sprinkling of water on the couples. There is also a laying on of hands, a passing of something from Rev. Moon to the couples. Perhaps that includes even some idea of holy ordinance. And there's an element of penance also, because the laying on of hands is an act to remove original sin.

*Dr. Sawatsky:* I think somebody was saying before that the movement would fail if Rev. Moon failed.

*Jonathan Wells:* What I was saying was that at the time of Jesus, human history went through a very critical stage. After Jesus died, the new age, which was Christianity, followed the pattern of what He accomplished and couldn't go beyond what He accomplished. So if this is the new age, and if Rev. Moon is the central figure, this new age will follow the pattern of that central figure and cannot transcend his accomplishments. But that's not to say that it would fail. Christianity didn't fail. It just didn't go as far as God wanted it to go.

*Dr. Bryant:* One of the difficulties here is the extent to which Jesus becomes a relevant and central figure for Unification, or the extent to which Jesus is superseded by Rev. Moon's conversations with Jesus and God.

*Mike Jenkins:* An understanding of Jesus is very central to my understanding of what I'm involved with today. Study of Jesus' life and teaching helps me to understand why Jesus came, the reason for His coming, and why He said He would return. Christology, the mission of the Second Advent, the purpose of the coming of the Messiah, all these things are essential to understanding the situation today.

*Klaus Lindner:* If we look at the Biblical accounts of Jesus, it's important to keep in mind that Jesus was not recognized. Many of the things that Jesus did are not normative for the establishment of the Kingdom of Heaven. For example, the concern for the poor that is portrayed in the gospels may be overstressed because the people who followed Jesus happened to be mostly poor people.

*Lloyd Eby:* In connection with the question about the relationship between Jesus and Rev. Moon, I think it's worth considering the parallel question: the relationship between Moses and Jesus. At the time of Jesus' life, some of the Jewish people came to Him and said they were followers of Moses. Jesus answered that if they were really followers of Moses, they would be followers of Him.

*Dr. Sawatsky:* Would you say that Moon is now the one who really determines who the true follower of God is? By analogy?

*Lloyd Eby:* Yes.

*Dr. Ward Wilson:* Can we just pick that one up a little bit? I have tried to determine if this is a Christian group or not, and part of the reason I've been wondering about that is that it seems to me that Christianity is of high import in the Unification movement, but possibly not necessarily. It would seem that you can come to know the Third Adam without necessarily knowing the Second Adam. You need to know the *position* of the Second Adam, but you need not know the person of the Second Adam. That is, you can come to the Third Adam as a Buddhist, a Hindu, or a Shintoist if you understand that Rev. Moon stands in the tradition of the Messiah. Is that right?

*Joe Stein:* I came to the Unification Church from a Jewish background. Part of the experience that I had in meeting the Unification Church seven and a half years ago came through an understanding of the mission of Jesus. This wasn't an understanding of the mission of Jesus as an intellectual concept or that Rev. Moon stood in the line of the prophets. No, the basis of Unification theology is an experiential relationship with God, with the heart of God. In order to understand the heart of God, we have to understand the heart of Jesus and that is not merely an intellectual understanding. We have to know and feel in ourselves what it is that Jesus felt through His life experience. Rev. Moon's revelation came on the foundation of Jesus' life and Jesus' experience, so Rev. Moon would be the last person to say that you can come without Jesus. So you can't come through the process of the Unification Church to a standard of the Kingdom of God or the Kingdom of Heaven on earth without the foundation of Jesus Christ. In becoming deeply connected with Rev. Moon at this time — a time in which God's Kingdom is imminent — we feel that we're also understanding the heart of Jesus Christ. It's not selling Jesus Christ short to become involved in the Unification Church and have a high esteem for Rev. Moon. The difficulty comes when Christians feel that we have supplanted Jesus with Rev. Moon. This causes a problem because people aren't aware of the depth of the relationship between Rev. Moon and Jesus Christ. We believe that that relationship with Jesus enables Rev. Moon to have his revelation and mission. If his mission is a mission to fulfill and, in a sense, to broaden what Jesus came to accomplish, then Rev. Moon would have to be completely one in heart, spirit and mind with God and with Jesus Christ himself. So, you could have been a Buddhist, or you could have been an atheist, or Hindu, or Confucianist, or Jew before you came into the Unification movement; but you have to come through Jesus' experience. You have to come through Christianity in that sense. You don't necessarily have to come through institutional Christianity, but you have to come through Christ.

*Diana Muxworthy:* From my own personal experience I would agree with Joe that Christianity and Jesus are central to our understanding. But the chronology of how they affect us may vary among the members.

# THE UNIFICATION MOVEMENT
# AND CHRISTIAN TRADITIONS

*Dr. Richardson:* Darrol has suggested that we talk about the relationship of Unification theology to the Christian tradition. I would like to make a suggestion. The theoretical question, it seems to me, is this: should one evaluate the things we're hearing today under Christology or ecclesiology? That's the question. I suppose one could argue the matter either way. Now, my inclination is to think that what we're dealing with here is not Christology, but ecclesiology. That is, we're dealing with the doctrine of the Holy Spirit, not the doctrine of Christ. Why is that the case? Because, essentially, what we're hearing is a theory about the organization of a visible community, and that's very much associated with categories of end-time and perfection which are traditionally Holy Spirit categories. I can see that to some extent this matter runs over into Christology, too. But, to put it another way, if one is asked to make a theological evaluation of the movement, I think that the fairest thing to do would be to think about it first of all under the doctrine of the Spirit, the doctrine of the Church. Thus we should think first about the communal aspect of it and not move immediately to talk about the figure of Rev. Moon and to whether he is or isn't a Christ figure, partly because, as Farley says, the Christological category is actually a secondary category. The important category is Adam, the New Adam.

My own theological reflection is something like this. I'm inclined to think that this group is within the Christian tradition. Unification theology is helping us in developing the doctrine of the Spirit in the Church, a kind of nineteenth and twentieth century problem tied up with the problem of eschatology. Speaking from a more orthodox perspective, the focus on the doctrine of the Spirit in the Church has always resulted in a certain inattention to, deformation of, its Christology. I would even grant this as a kind of historical point. But Unification's whole doctrine of creation is pretty orthodox. If you think of all the things said today, you'll remember that we didn't talk about Christology very much at all. We talked about the doctrine of creation and about the doctrine of the Church. We jumped over Christology in order to talk about these two things. Now that's my view of the matter. While I don't think the Unification Church is orthodox, I don't think they're unorthodox either. The reason why they're not unorthodox is because there are many undeveloped issues concerning the relationship between Christology and ecclesiology.

*Dr. Vander Goot:* But you said nothing about the *contents* of their ecclesiology or the *contents* of the doctrine of the Holy Spirit. You're judging the system quite abstractly in terms of certain formal structures: how the doctrine of the Holy Spirit is related to the doctrine of the Church, and how the doctrine of the Church is related to the doctrine of creation. And judged on that level, it seems to me you couldn't say it's either orthodox or unorthodox. In other words, it seems to me you have to engage in a rather abstract theological analysis to answer the question of whether or not Unification is within the orthodox tradition or not.

*Dr. Bryant:* Let's not resolve this whole question before various participants have spoken on it. It seems to me that the question of Unification and its relation to the Christian tradition is an open question. It can be evaluated in a number of different ways. I think it would be interesting to see the different ways in which the various participants here would begin to approach that question.

*Dr. Klaaren:* It strikes me that it's goofy to pursue the question of Unification being orthodox or nonorthodox in relation to the Christian tradition. In the first place, things are orthodox or not orthodox in relation to what's true. The truth that comes from God is not first of all in relation to the tradition. Secondly, we run into problems when we talk, as Christians, about the Unification movement as orthodox or not with reference to *the* Christian tradition. There are *many* Christian traditions. I mean, what Christian theologian today thinks solely in terms of *the* Christian tradition? He's always grappling with many Christian traditions. And one of the most interesting things about the Unification movement is that they immediately take *all* the traditions and put them all together. (laughter)

*Dr. Bryant:* Let's move beyond the formal kind of analysis

and see if anyone has anything to say. I guess I'll begin. One of the things that interests me about this group is that I see them as offering a particular specification and interpretation of a mystery of the Christian faith: the mystery of the resurrection of the body. And quite contrary to some of the other opinions that have been expressed here, I'm intrigued by the explicitly "sexual" interpretation both of the Fall and the restoration. I see the Unification interpretation as an attempt to answer a question that is an open question within the Christian tradition. What do we mean by "the resurrection of the body?" This is a question that the Christian tradition has dealt with, a question that is included in the lexicon of Christian theological issues. Here in Unification's idea of the "physical restoration" we have a very specific answer to that question.

*Rev. Calitis:* Are you referring to St. Paul's statement that in Christ we shall all have spiritual bodies, and saying that the Unification Church specifies what that body is?

*Dr. Bryant:* No, not a spiritual body, but the "resurrected body." In the New Testament, that idea is related to Jesus as the first fruit of redemption. In the story of the resurrection appearances, the New Testament talks about Jesus having a resurrected body, a transformed body for which there were no analogues. One element of New Testament theology is the belief that Jesus is the first fruit of the resurrection of the whole Creation. What we have here is a proposal about a timetable for the whole divine economy: a proposal about a way to understand this general "resurrection of the body" that is one of the characteristics, or one of the signs, of the dawning of the Kingdom of God.

*Dr. Sawatsky:* It is more than a timetable for the resurrection. We're moving here into a millennium that finds resurrection in others besides Jesus.

*Dr. Bryant:* Yes, of course. But the question for the Christian tradition is: what does the resurrection of the body mean? In the Christian tradition we affirm that Jesus was resurrected from the dead and that he gets a "new body." In the New Testament we read about his having a body that walks through walls, etc. I would understand that as a Christian mystery. We affirm the resurrection, but we don't know how it is to be accomplished. This is, I think, a very characteristic Christian theological move. In the New Testament, Jesus' resurrection is related to an eschatological notion of this being one of the manifestations, the first fruit, of the Kingdom. In Unification theology we have a specific kind of interpretation of this mystery. The fact that Unification theology offers an interpretation of a Christian mystery relates it to all Christian traditions.

*Dr. Klaaren:* But in the Christian traditions we find the resurrected reality of Jesus' presence understood in different ways. Catholics say that the resurrected Jesus is present in the sacramental system and in the Mass. Mainline Protestants say that the reality of the resurrected Jesus is present most pointedly in the preaching of the Word. And a couple of Mennonite Brethren that I know say that the reality of the resurrected Jesus is present in their very own group when they gather together. They would say that when two of us or three of us are gathered in the name of Jesus, He is here. So here are three differently believed and practiced ways of specifying the reality of the resurrected Jesus. The role of a Christian theologian is to deal with the manyness of that reality. I don't know much about the Unification Church yet, but it seems to me that they are trying to put together a whole lot of things, to integrate a number of traditions. Now whether or not Unification theology gets to the point of specifying a mystery in a satisfactory way, I don't know.

*Dr. Bryant:* I'm not denying other specifications of this mystery. I'm saying that this is one way in which Unification theology is related to the Christian tradition. Like these other traditions, it offers a specific interpretation of a particular doctrinal issue. And that doesn't mean that any of the others are false or that this one's true. I'm giving a general answer to the question about the relationship of this movement to the Christian tradition. This would be one element of my answer to that question.

*Dr. Sawatsky:* I think that what we have here is a definition of the phrase from the Lord's Prayer: "Thy Kingdom come, on Earth as it is in Heaven." The gathering together in Jesus' name of the Mennonites, the preaching of the Word of the Lutherans, etc., are but signs of this Coming, or pointers in the direction of the ultimate millennium that is to dawn. It seems to me that it is within this context that one needs to understand what's happening here with Unification. In Unification theology we have a specificity about what that millennium is going to be, of what it's going to be in terms of the new order, the new people, the perfection which goes even beyond the Christ. Mormonism has a similar notion. I'd like to know more about the geography of this Kingdom, of this millennium. Where is the New Jerusalem? I think that this has all kinds of implications for social and political ethics, world affairs, and so on.

*Rev. Calitis:* Could I pursue the point previous to the question of geography? You, Darrol, said that in Unification theology there's a kind of specificity that the Lutherans for example either haven't had or have avoided in relation to belief in the resurrection of the body. It is true that the Lutheran tradition has always put the resurrection at a distance. The belief in justification by faith really pushes away and spiritualizes the idea of the "resurrection of the body." In the Lutheran tradition we make a virtue of the problem, and say there's an advantage to not specifying in this way because in fact the end time isn't here. We say that you can't jump too fast to specificity because this cuts down on the spiritual possibilities. What we're really doing in this life is expanding the spiritual possibilities of our relationship to God rather than narrowing down the options.

*Dr. Sawatsky:* In my tradition — Mennonite — I can see all kinds of similarities with the Unification Church in its concern for specificity and concreteness. We want specificity. We want to *see* that restored community. And if we don't see that community, we're copping out.

*Rev. Calitis:* Well of course, and that's the power of it. I mean anyone who can point a finger at the community and say "there it is" has a tremendous advantage. Whereas Lutherans don't know where the Kingdom is! (laughter)

And the other question, somewhat linked to that is: where is the physical regeneration, or where does it occur? It occurs in Jesus, who is God and man. Jesus is the physical fact, the incarnation being the one instance where the injury occasioned by sin is overcome.

*Dr. Clark:* How can Unification theology be orthodox if it hasn't a Christology that's in any way in keeping with what all Christians were supposed to think after the fourth century?

*Dr. Richardson:* First of all, it isn't quite clear to me that they don't. That is, they would say that the *Divine Principle* is still developing and that their Christology is very much focused in terms of the question of ecclesiology. That's what I think. But I don't want to belabor this point. If I were to argue the matter I'd put it this way: I'd say that the Unification Church is a kind of American millennialist, social gospel religion. Now the American millennialist social gospel tradition played down the deity of Jesus, the doctrine of two natures and all those fourth century notions, and instead spoke about Jesus as a man who was trying to fulfill God's purposes for creation. The preaching of the Kingdom of God, relating directly to the prophetic tradition, spoke about a salvation taking place on earth. They saw that the work of Jesus was to establish the Kingdom. That's Rauschenbusch, right? Christology is transformed into ecclesiology. The work of the church is building the Kingdom of God on earth. Now, what I see is that you read Walter Rauschenbusch, and you've got the theology for the Unification Church. That's of course an amusing overstatement. (laughter) But really, the heart of Unification theology is American social gospel.

*Dr. Vander Goot:* You're always thinking abstractly, in terms of common structures. But you have got to look at the content.

*Dr. Richardson:* Oh, the content. Listen, the content of our entire discussion this morning is about the Church in terms of building Christian families which is right there in Horace Bushnell and is right there, by the way, in Michigan, and is right there at the heart of your Dutch Reformed uncle who said that the whole of the Ten Commandments is summarized in one: "Thou Shalt Not Commit Adultery." (much laughter)

*Dr. Vander Goot:* You could start from there too, because you could take one element from the Christian theological content and say, "Look, it's present here; it plays a central ordering role here, as it does in other forms of Christian theology." But if you take the Unification orientation as a total system, then it seems to me not even problematic for the Unification people to say that this is not orthodox. Are they even concerned about this question? I think it's a goofy question.

*Dr. Richardson:* But the question has been asked and I have made these points just for that reason. It isn't a goofy question; it's a very practical question. If I were an historian of religions I would look at the Unification Movement and I would say, well, it looks very much like the Mormons, and it looks very much like the American, liberal, social gospel movement, and it looks very much like certain things in the Great Awakening, and it has connections with the Shaker community and Oneida community. I'm not saying there's perfect overlap, but it's related to these. It's related to the millennialist tradition. What is the practical purpose of saying this? Well, after all, one wants to say this because, to come down to gut level, the Faith and Order Commission of the National Council of Churches has attacked the Unification Church as not a Christian group, as not at all related to the Christian tradition. That attack is part of the general strategy to say that Unification is not even a religion at all: it's a cult, and these people are not entitled to religious freedom.

*Dr. Vander Goot:* But then, the strategy is wrong. Unification might not be part of the Christian tradition, but who can persecute it for that?

*Dr. Richardson:* Oh, well, then, Henry, on that point, I must say I have enough theological sophistication to find it very amusing that the Faith and Order Commission of the National Council of Churches can suddenly jump around waving Chalcedon in the face of the Unification Church, saying they're bad, bad people. For years we've been hearing that you can't believe in Chalcedon. The duplicity and audacity of this move by the Faith and Order Commission is incredible.

*Dr. Vander Goot:* In a sense, I love it, because if you could just get the National Council of Churches to type its own members by the criteria by which it judges the Unification Church, we might save the Christian tradition. (laughter)

*Dr. Sawatsky:* You're really talking about the control that the liberal religious establishment has on North American society. That's the problem, it seems to me. There's an attempt to identify a particular Christian Protestant orientation with religion and with Americans. That's the issue.

*Dr. Vander Goot:* I think that's right on a practical level. And I would oppose that. But at a strictly theological level, it's no problem for me to say that Unification theology is unorthodox.

*Dr. Bryant:* You mean it's not Christian Reformed? What do you mean?

*Dr. Vander Goot:* Well, that's a caricature. I don't see why it's problematical to say that something is not orthodox. That doesn't mean that the conversation ends; that doesn't mean that you can't continue to have contact with another person; that doesn't mean anything like that at all. I'm just making distinctions. The Christian tradition is something, but it's not everything. For example, in the Christian tradition it is not possible to believe that God made the world out of pre-existent matter. Nor is it possible within the Christian tradition to say that evil is one side of God. Or to say that from eternity there coexist two principles, one good, one evil. These are not possibilities within the Christian tradition. You've just got to make certain discriminations.

*Dr. Richardson:* All the things you've offered are categories drawn from the doctrine of creation. You define Christianity in terms of orthodox statements concerning the doctrine of creation. Somebody else would define the Christian tradition in terms of orthodox statements concerning Christology. Now what I find so interesting is that within the Unification movement theological questions are more open than they are for you. I agree with you that whether they're orthodox or not shouldn't be decisive of their fate. But what I can't accept is the insistence on "orthodoxy" or confessional definitiveness in relation to eschatology and to the big questions that the Christian tradition *doesn't yet have answers for.* So in a sense, the orthodoxy or unorthodoxy of Unification theology can't be adjudicated yet because certain theological work has to be done within the Christian tradition as a whole. When you have a Lutheran view of the Kingdom, and a Mennonite view of the Kingdom and an Edwardian view of the Kingdom, and a Catholic view of the Kingdom that are all uncertain, and when we don't know if we believe in a Pope, or Presbyteries, or this or that, then it seems to me that the whole question of the form of Christian life in the Kingdom and what the Kingdom is to be is completely open to discussion within the Christian tradition. You would agree there, wouldn't you?

*Dr. Vander Goot:* I certainly would with respect to the doctrine of the Holy Spirit and the doctrine of the Last Days where there's great latitude.

*Dr. Clark:* I'd like to reply to Herb on the Christology question. That part about Liberal Protestants is clearly wrong. You can change the language; people in the nineteenth or twentieth century aren't necessarily going to affirm the doctrine in the same language as the Council of Chalcedon. But can you have anyone arguing that Jesus failed, as I understand these people do, and still count them within the Christian tradition? Can you be a Christian and say Jesus failed?

*Dr. Richardson:* Listen, that is just not right. Lutherans, for example, would say Jesus failed and that it is in his failure that we see the deeper purpose of God.

*Rev. Calitis:* Wait! Isn't the Lutheran position that we are justified by the death of Christ on the Cross? Admittedly, that's paradoxical, but the crucifixion is a "success."

*Dr. Richardson:* Unification theology holds that Jesus succeeded in just that sense. I don't understand why everyone gets so excited about the idea that Jesus failed. I've talked with many different groups of Christians. They all agree that the precise sense in which the Unification Church teaches Jesus failed is precisely what the Christian churches teach, namely, that the purpose of Jesus was to establish the Kingdom of God on earth at the time of His ministry and that purpose was not realized. Henry, was or wasn't that His purpose?

*Dr. Vander Goot:* Yes, and He did fulfill His purpose.

*Dr. Richardson:* How did He do it?

*Dr. Vander Goot:* He died His death on the Cross. He accomplished our justification.

*Dr. Richardson:* But the justification of believers and the establishment of the Kingdom of God on earth are two different things.

*Dr. Vander Goot:* Not for Luther. This is where you are not acknowledging the fine points of theological interpretation.

*Dr. Richardson:* Is this the view that *you* hold, Henry?

*Dr. Vander Goot:* Yes. I'd say this for myself, too.

*Dr. Richardson:* Well, okay. I would say that it's perfectly alright to say that; but then what is the purpose of the Second Coming to which Paul and all the early Christians looked forward? And isn't that Second Coming related to something more that is going to be done by the Christ?

*Dr. Vander Goot:* You can't talk about the fact that the Kingdom is not completely accomplished as a failure.

*Lynn Kim:* In the Unification movement, we never ever say Jesus failed. That's put on us from outside.

*Dr. Bryant:* What's the Unification view?

*Lynn Kim:* The Unification view is that Jesus came with a mission to fulfill, but that mission wasn't completed. That's what necessitates the Second Coming. We don't ever talk of Jesus as a failure.

*Dr. Clark:* But you do have a new messianic figure in Rev. Moon. Now, you're not saying Rev. Moon is a new incarnation of Jesus, are you? Is that what you're saying?

*Dr. Bryant:* Before someone answers that, can I make a proposal? I think this might help us in our difficulty about the question of what would constitute an orthodox Christology. I think the question of Christology is complex, very complex. It involves a range of things, many of which are open to dispute and can be articulated in a number of different ways. I would take it that there would be only one thing that one would have to say to be a part of the orthodox tradition, and that is that "Jesus is true man and true God."

*Jonathan Wells:* That's exactly what the Unification Church teaches.

*Dr. Bryant:* Other aspects of Christology are disputed. We know that there are different Christologies within the Christian tradition. The only thing one must hold, I think, to be orthodox — and that is simply as a guide, a rule to be observed in our reflection upon the person of Jesus — is the formula "true man, true God." But what its implications are for various aspects of Christological doctrine, is an open question. That would be my view. So I would allow that Unification could be within the orthodox tradition of Christology if it affirms Jesus as true man and true God.

*Dr. Sawatsky:* But clarify this. I take it that the Unification Church says that Jesus is true God and true man. So at that level Unification is within the Christian tradition. But what about the level of piety and practice? For example, do you pray to Jesus?

*Lloyd Eby:* I pray to God.

*Dr. Sawatsky:* But do you pray to Jesus?

*Lokesh Mazumdar:* Well, in the sense that I can pray to the spirit world in general, I might be able to talk to Jesus; but I don't know if I could call that prayer.

*Klaus Lindner:* We could pray in the name of Jesus.

*Lynn Kim:* Jesus taught us to pray "Our Father, Who art in Heaven."

*Christa Dabeck:* He taught us to pray in His name.

*Jonathan Wells:* Can I tell you word for word what we teach about Jesus? This is in our first basic lecture that we teach to anybody that wants to learn about our movement. When we come to explaining the meaning of the First Blessing, which means individual perfection, we say Jesus was perfect in the sense that He was one with God, which comes straight from the Bible: "I and my Father are one — you see me, you see the Father."

*Dr. Clark:* But Jesus said, "I and the Father are one." That's different from saying that Jesus *was* perfect.

*Jonathan Wells:* Well, we're defining perfection by that phrase "I and my Father are one." I'm just telling you what I teach in an introductory lecture. Then we say Jesus, a perfect man, has deity. A perfect man is one with God and has deity. There's another term we use.

*Tom Selover:* You can say that as the body is a reflection of the mind, so Jesus was the "second God." Now, that doesn't mean that He's exactly the same as the first, but that Jesus is God in a very valid and complete sense that's not the same as God the Father, Creator. Jesus is a human being also. So that's the way that we say Jesus is the second God; but He's not God Himself, which means God as Creator.

*Jonathan Wells:* That's all explanation, though. What I was telling you was word for word the Unification position.

*Dr. Clark:* It's still coming out somehow Rev. Moon is "more God" than Jesus.

*Students in a Chorus:* No. No.

*Christa Dabeck:* You have to understand Jesus in relation to the will of God. Let me explain. Jesus was really completely united with God's will . . .

*Dr. Clark:* That's a heresy. If that's your definition of the divinity of Jesus, then it's heresy.

*Dr. Richardson:* But it's only an early Church historian who would know that. (laughter) Which heresy is that?

*Dr. Clark:* I mean, *any* believer can be united with the will of God. So what's the specific difference with Jesus?

*Lynn Kim:* Which Christian has been perfectly in tune with the will of God?

*Dr. Bryant:* Hold it. We jumped on Christa and accused her of heresy without hearing her out. She barely got half a sentence out before we told her she was a heretic. (laughter) We don't even have an idea of what it was that she wanted to say.

*Christa Dabeck:* I wanted to say that each person has, in God's providence, a position, and that God chooses people according to their qualifications for that position. And Jesus' position is to bring people back to God. He united with the will of God in this way. He reached complete oneness with the will of God, which was an understanding of His providence. And you say that there are many Christians who are united with the will of God. But it depends on how you understand the will of God. Jesus had — and this is what is special about Him — the knowledge of God's providence and the willingness to fulfill it.

*Dr. Clark:* That's still not a qualitative difference. I want to hear something that points to a qualitative difference between Jesus and the community of believers. That's the crux of the Christological question.

*Lynn Kim:* I'm not sure what you want. We say that Jesus was a special creation of God. We say that He was created without original sin. So, He was special.

*Dr. Vander Goot:* You say that He was created?

*Lynn Kim:* No, He was begotten. (laughter)

*Dr. Richardson:* Isn't this funny? Henry is usually attacking me for using Greek categories and now, all of a sudden, he is wrapped up in Greek categories. But seriously, shouldn't we allow people to explore new theological categories? Obviously, the effort here is to find categories which focus not on commonality of nature or substance, but on communion of will. In Unification theology it seems that the focus is on the will as the fundamental matter to be understood. I think that's an interesting enterprise.

*Lloyd Eby:* I believe that the *Divine Principle* teaches that not just anybody could have taken the position of the Messiah. He wasn't just a carpenter's son. He was a special creation, created sinless specifically to be the Messiah. But once the Messiah is here every man has the potential for becoming one with the Messiah, one with God and a true child of God.

*Jonathan Wells:* Wait a minute. I'd like to ask another question. What is the orthodox Christian position on Christology? I studied the Ecumenical councils and I've read the doctrines, but I've also heard about five different versions talking with Christians out on the streets. I'm not sure how to reply to a question about whether or not we are orthodox on Christology because I've heard so many versions of Christology.

*Dr. Bryant:* Well, I think it is perfectly obvious that we are not going to solve this question today. It is also perfectly clear that when you get a group of Christian theologians together it is hard, if not impossible, to achieve a consensus on what constitutes the main lines of Christian faith, let alone Christian theology. One should, I suppose, be very careful about denying that a group is part of the Christian tradition if it understands itself in relation to that tradition. It is also clear that there are differences of opinion on this matter among Unification people, about specific doctrinal questions. However, it does seem to me that the *Divine Principle* understands itself in relation to the Christian tradition even though it also understands itself to go beyond the Christian Scriptures at certain points. At this point, however, we have to break for lunch.

# THE MILLENNIAL LANDSCAPE:
# POLITICS OF THE KINGDOM

*Dr. Sawatsky:* I'm concerned that we have not touched on one realm of thought: the geography and the politics of the Unification Church. I'm not sure it is that important, but it's been in a lot of headlines.

*Dr. Richardson:* Yes, this element is terribly important. Any discussion that we have that doesn't go into this remains very abstract. We've been so much into this doctrine of intimate sexuality and marriage that one almost wonders if the rest of the world is real. I would propose that we get to this aspect of Unification theology.

*Dr. Bryant:* Would someone be willing to give us an overview of either the geography or the millennial timetable? We touched on that, to a certain extent, in the discussion of the notion of the Third Adam. But it's more than that, I take it. "The Kingdom of Heaven on Earth" — I keep seeing it underlined in some of the material that I've read. Can someone describe that part?

*Farley Jones:* Part of our concept of history is that of the central person, a central figure, and not only a central figure, but a central family, and then a central nation. We conceive of Israel as the central nation at the time of Jesus, and from that nation God's Kingdom was to spread out to the world. In our time, we see Korea in that role, in a parallel position to Israel two thousand years ago. We see the resolution of the conflict between North and South Korea as critical to the resolution of the conflict on a larger level between Communism and Democracy. We see that Korea is a symbolic prototype of the larger conflict, the larger division in the world. And we see the resolution there as part of the larger resolution that God is working for in building a harmonious and unified world on earth, one family on earth. Others might like to add something.

*Lynn Kim:* Very important in our viewpoint is America's position. This goes back to the idea that if Jesus had established a family and if His nation had accepted Him, then the Christians would have converted Rome. We see America as in a similar position to Rome, and Korea in a similar position to Israel. In America or from America a world like the Kingdom of God will come. America was especially created and ordained by God as a Christian nation. The basic mentality, the basic cultural heritage of America is a Christian heritage uniting all the different Christian traditions. So America's divine purpose or mission is to become a model for the Kingdom of God on earth which represents all the peoples of the world and all the different religions of the world. We are, in a sense, a microcosm of our world. It would be here that we could set an example for a united world. We have a United States, and now we want to have a united world. So America is very important, and that's why Rev. Moon's working so hard here in America.

*Dr. Bryant:* But is this a Christian nation? Can you specify that any further? Is there something peculiar about the very political institutions of America and other structural features of America that in themselves have some religious significance? Or is yours a spiritualized notion of America as forerunner of a new world which draws all the peoples of the world together?

*Lynn Kim:* I think in terms of the original purpose for the family of America. If you look at the nations of the world, you don't see a nation that was conceived for the purpose of God as America purports to be. America is a nation that was conceived as a haven of religious liberty, and its motto is "In God We Trust." When we talk about America's position in God's providence and the world today, we see that America is far from being a truly Christian nation. But we do see America as potentially a Christian nation. It's been said that we are indeed a melting pot of many different nations. So the idea of uniting this world and making one world that can communicate beyond cultural barriers, beyond the kind of barriers that exist in Europe and around the world, can be made actual in America. In this sense, America is a microcosm of what could happen in the world.

*Dr. Bryant:* But that's part of the problem, isn't it? Why take these images? For example, you mentioned the melting pot one. That's one that those of us who have lived in Canada for years have come to know is not particularly admirable or noble and certainly not a divine notion about how the Kingdom is to be understood. I think that Canadians have a much richer notion in that we talk about the Canadian mosaic. Canada incorporates *different* cultural traditions. The melting pot idea moves in another direction. The melting pot idea assumes that there is a single type of person that you become out of this interaction.

*Linda Mitchell:* I don't think that our idea takes away from the individuality of cultures at all. Our idea is one of being able to exist as one harmonious unit. As individuals in the Kingdom we will each manifest a different kind of personality because of our individuality. So can nations. We are concerned to be able to transcend the barriers that we see causing a lot of problems in our world today. We are trying to overcome national barriers, but at the same time we want to preserve the uniqueness that is part of the beauty of God.

*Lloyd Eby:* To make some sense out of what's been said, I think we need to make a distinction between a nation which occupies a providential role and a nation which is perfect. There would be no claim here, under any circumstances, that America or any of the democratic powers represent any kind of perfection. One can speak of fallen people and by extrapolation you can also speak of fallen societies and fallen nations. We would see all of the people and all of the nations in the world as fallen people and nations. Just as within the group of fallen people there are some who are Christian and some who are anti-Christian, we would also see that some of the nations are in a representative position which is, as compared to the other, demonic, and some representative of the position which is less demonic or tending more toward the ideal. And we could say that America, for example, occupies in the world today the role which the Roman Empire occupied at the time of the advent of Christ. If Jesus had not been crucified, if He had been able to succeed in whatever it was that He was trying to do, then, on the foundation of the Israelite nation, He could have gone on, He and His followers, to Rome. And then Rome could have been used as a vehicle to transmit His message, His saving work, to the rest of the world. Rome had the facilities, the roads, the commercial network, etc.

*Rev Calitis:* Isn't that exactly what happened with Constantine?

*Lloyd Eby:* Yes, but that is a subsidiary question. After Jesus was crucified, Christianity was able to use the Roman Empire to accomplish that end.

*Dr. Richardson:* I take it that you're contrary to most church historians: you like Constantine, and you like Charlemagne.

*Lloyd Eby:* We would say of them, too, that they were fallen people. Yet they had a certain providence to effect; to some extent they succeeded, and to some extent they failed. And in a sense it doesn't matter whether or not we like them.

*Dr. Sawatsky:* There's no "Fall" of the church?

*Lloyd Eby:* Yes, one could speak that way. One could point to particular times or particular events in which something like a "Fall" occurred. We could point to America, for example, and say the introduction of slavery in America represented a "Fall" for America. Nevertheless, we would see America's role today as important. We say that there is something unique about America, its institutions, its structure, its history, its personality; and those unique things represent at least the possiblity of something which now can be realized for the whole world. It doesn't mean that they have, in fact, done that, but it means that they represent it.

*Dr. Bryant:* Can you give an example of what those institutions would be? Is it republican government versus parliamentary government?

*Lynn Kim:* Not necessarily political institutions. But things like freedom of religion, freedom of the press.

*Dr. Bryant:* How is that a Christian idea? How is the idea of religious liberty as it originates in the United States a Christian idea?

*Lynn Kim:* I don't think it has to be Christian. The point is that it has to serve God's providence, and in this case, I think it does.

*Dr. Richardson:* I remember some time ago I spoke to a minister about this, and he said it sounds like a high school student's understanding of history. And I said that it's true, it is a high school student's understanding of history. But if you go back to the Old Testament and you look at the understanding of history of Israel it's precisely the same kind of thing. I suspect, for example, that when the people of Israel came out of Egypt, maybe Moses and two other people thought that this represented some kind of divine providence. People came out of Egypt for all kinds of reasons. But seen from the point of view of the providential import of that event, it does represent some major providential step. Similarly, the foundation of America, although it was founded for all kinds of reasons and people who came here came here for all kinds of reasons, nevertheless, from the point of view of providence, it represents this kind of step.

I suppose that more to the point in relation to America would be the vision in America of building the Kingdom of God on earth. Doesn't this come much closer to your thing? Religious freedom seems more peripheral. But another matter interests me: wouldn't you want to present your view of the importance of America more dialectically? That is, America is important because America represents Abel to the Soviet Union's Cain. In a more dialectical view of history, the importance of America in world history is that America emerges as a protagonist of one point of view at the same time that a protagonist of another point of view is emerging in the historical process. America is important because it has tremendous economic, political and military power that can serve as a counterweight to the tremendous economic, military and political power that one finds in the Soviet Union. So the important thing America represents is democracy, although that's a symbol rather than a reality. But I would think that, in a sense, the importance of America can't be abstracted merely from the realm of religious liberty and the idea of the Kingdom of God on earth, but has to be seen as a counterweight to Communism.

*Farley Jones:* I think that is essentially how we understand the significance of America; more, much more, than any of the other things we've talked about so far, we understand America as a counterweight to Communism.

*Dr. Bryant:* America as the counterweight to Communism? I don't know if I get that. Do you mean that in economic terms or what kind of terms?

*Lynn Kim:* I think one of the unfortunate things is that America has sought to counteract Communism either through economic or political means: dishing out military weapons and dishing out economic aid, but never investing itself as a Christian people really serving other nations. We've given things, but we've never given of our hearts. We've not borne witness to the Christian faith that's supposed to be our heritage. Sure, we have missionaries. But if we would fulfill the purpose of the blessings of America, which were not given just for Americans to enjoy, but which were to be used to raise up the rest of the world, then, in a sense, America would take on a parental role to the rest of the world. Not parental in the sense that "We're superior to you, you're our little kids," but "You have something, and we will help you develop so that we can raise up the level of the entire world community, and so establish this on a God-centered foundation." We're one of the few nations on earth that has the potential to do that. And if we should counterpose it to the aggressive spread of Communism, America could be the foundation, a landing pad, for the Messiah.

*Dr. Clark:* What do you do with the whole notion of Church/State separation in America? Talking about America as a Christian nation is very peculiar.

*Lynn Kim:* There shouldn't be one church, e.g. the Presbyterian Church. The Presbyterians shouldn't take over the government. We're talking about the Christian spirit which is the spirit of belief in God and service to mankind.

*Jonathan Wells:* Let's go back and talk about Constantine. In our view, as I understand it, had Constantine been able to perfect the proper kind of marriage between political and religious institutions, or political and religious impulses, and had that promise been carried out, then one would have had a united Europe. One would have had a Europe which represented something approximating a godly Kingdom. And it is because that wasn't carried out that one had conflicts. Because of all those failures, then, it became necessary to separate the political and the religious institutions. But the reason it became necessary to separate them wasn't there from the beginning. It became necessary to separate them only when the failures intervened. And so the task today is to rejoin them in a way in which this genuine relation between religion and politics can be realized.

*Lloyd Eby:* You can talk about this in a religious way, and you can talk about it in a political way. But that's artificial. It's not as if we want to make the church identical with the state. But the purpose of the church as a structure, as a way of doing things, and the purpose of the state, as a way of doing things, are somehow involved in the salvation process. That is most fundamental to what's going on in the world. Maybe we can get around to the question of whether or not there is a Messiah on the national level. That's something else again. That's not America; that's not anything we have right now.

*Dr. Bryant:* It's not? It sounds like it is. A number of you heard me say this before. It sounds to me like you fall into that confusion that seems to have plagued American millennial movements from the beginning: the confusion of the millennium with this particular country. American institutions and policies are somehow raised above other nations and other institutions and other policies, and do not seem to be subject to the same kinds of deformities and ambiguities and tragedies that characterize other political institutions.

*Lloyd Eby:* There is the possibility that we can make that

mistake, also. But we don't actually. You see, built into our acceptance of America in this role is at the same time an acceptance of America as a fallen nation. Similarly, built into our acceptance of Christianity as the major transmitter of God's providence is also the acceptance of Christianity as a fallen religion. None of these things represent the ideal. They represent only approximations of it.

*Dr. Bryant:* That seems to be a technical point, since it seems clear that America is less fallen than other nations.

*Lloyd Eby:* Yes, but that doesn't confer rights, it only confers obligations. In other words, when we talk about chosen people, or a chosen nation, or a chosen individual, it's not to elevate that entity to a privileged level, but to point out that God expects that entity to serve the rest of the world. That's what America should be doing with her wealth.

*Dr. Sawatsky:* I hear about four or five different things. But the immediate analogy is not between Israel as a chosen nation and America as a chosen nation, as, for example, in Robert Bellah's "civil religion," but the immediate analogy is between Israel as a chosen nation and Korea as a chosen nation. And I'm very big on Korea, because I'm very against America as a chosen nation. (laughter)

*Rev. Calitis:* So it has to be put off in the Far East somewhere.

*Dr. Sawatsky:* A small, impotent chosen nation.

*Dr. Richardson:* That's right, I think that's a point. You know, that's even in the *Divine Principle:* that a chosen nation needs to be a small, impotent nation. So when one is talking about America, then, as a chosen nation, the first thing you've already broken is the new Israel myth, the Bellah thing. Okay, then, what's essential when one talks about America? The word "chosen" is probably wrong. Probably you mean to speak of America's task or responsibility. The difference between Bellah, it seems to me, and Rev. Moon is that at least while you glorify America, and I think overglorify it, you're talking about America in an international context. You say many things about America, but you move from the nation to the world. You have a vision of an international community that America must serve. Now, I'm not sure that I find this completely satisfactory. But I do think that the internationalism of the theology has to be stated along with the nationalism as an equally weighty part.

However, having gotten over Jonathan Edwards and the Great Awakening into a kind of Catholic view of reality, it's hard for me to come back and ask: do particular nations have responsibilities in international development that are special? I guess they do. I guess I would say that America does have special responsibilities. I can talk about the nation as having, as a nation, moral responsibility. And now the question is: does it make any sense for me to go on from there and say that God has larger historical purposes such that if America has moral responsibilities in the international order, perhaps one should concede that these may be related in some sense to God's purposes? I'm inclined to go that way, though I feel very uneasy about it because I tend to agree with the Catholic tendency to drop off that type of philosophy of history from my Christianity. How does this strike you, Lokesh and Klaus? You are not Americans.

*Lokesh Mazumdar:* Well, I actually believed that America was a very special nation before I came here. When I did come here I found America was special, far beyond my expectations. So even before I joined the Unification Church and adopted many of its views, I was convinced that if any substantial movement came, it would come from this country. And there are many reasons for this. I don't see America as ideal. Neither do I see the ideal life in India, nor in Russia or anywhere else. But I do think that if an idea or an ideology were able to come and take root, it would do so far more easily here, within this structure. So as a jumping off point to the Kingdom of Heaven, I think that America is a very qualified nation, far more qualified than any other nation I can think of. And, of course, it makes a great deal of sense to me that America will be a kind of servant nation to the world. This is very obvious in many ways. I say this partly because of economics, partly because of the people. The nature of the people in America is, I believe, a nature that leans toward wanting to help other people. There's a lot of bungling and there are a lot of crazy things, but there's also that very outstanding nature. I don't mean to downgrade any other nationality, but I do think that America is the most international country that I've ever seen. It is very open.

*Dr. Richardson:* This is just incredible, they've all been brainwashed. (much laughter)

*Linda Mitchell:* I think I can state a different viewpoint. When I met the Unification Church, the nation I hated the most in the entire cosmos was America. I left America and was living in Italy, and I became an anti-American. My friends and I were like Hemingway expatriates. We wouldn't speak English, not even if our lives depended on it. Looking back on that time, I think that I realized then that what America purported to be — a Christian nation, a nation that was giving and serving and all this kind of stuff

— wasn't true. I saw the reality of our country, and it made me sick to my stomach. And I thought, "Well, I can't change it, so I'm just going to leave and go someplace else where they don't say one thing and do something different." When the Unification Church talked about America and America's role, I thought, "Oh, yuk." I just couldn't relate to that at all. So it's taken me a long time and a lot of serious prayer to come around to realizing the potential that America has: that God can use her and requires things of America that aren't actually a part of the American nation now. I think anybody who has lived outside of America has to have that same kind of feeling. But I can see the potential that America has partly because it's a nation without a culture, in a sense. When you go to Italy or Japan you find such an established culture. Trying to do anything new is like pounding against rock. But in America you can just blow and things change. So America has a potential since people are more open-minded, more ready to try something new that's better than what already is.

*Dr. Richardson:* That's reasonable, I think. But that's really saying that the potential for America is not in its greatness, but in its unformedness. Think about the deprogramming thing. How ironic it is that the American Civil Liberties Union, who are so ardently committed to an essentially secular state, are defending theocratic groups like the Unification Church and Hare Krishnas. There's something about the contradictory tensions or forces in America that makes it possible, it seems to me, for new ideas, for a new religious movement, to take root here.

*Dr. Sawatsky:* Isn't there a difference between potentiality and chosenness? Potentiality I'm ready to grant, but chosenness is more problematic.

*Lloyd Eby:* I don't know that there's as much difference as we usually think. I think that when you say chosen, you also say potentiality. I say this since "chosenness" is dependent on the response, on what you do with your freedom. And the idea of chosen is "chosen to fulfill." Now, that doesn't mean that America will succeed. It means that America has the potential and the opportunity to succeed.

*Lynn Kim:* If America weren't able to fulfill the mission that America has of being God's springboard, that mission could easily transfer, and may still yet transfer, to a different nation that will in fact fulfill the mission.

*Lloyd Eby:* This chosen nation idea is often misunderstood. Some think that if you're chosen, you have the liberty to do things that other people don't get a chance to do. Actually, what it means

is that you get beat on. (laughter) Look at Israel. What does
"chosen" mean to Israel? It means a pain in the neck.

*Dr. Sawatsky:* Israel finally identifies its political destiny with
the coming of the Kingdom and that is their fundamental mistake.
And you're still making the structural mistake that Israel made:
the mistake that the Kingdom is specially present in one nation and
absent or less present in others.

*Dr. Richardson:* But you see, that's so contrary to the whole
Unification movement. You look around and see already an inter-
national and mixed group. It is not an American Legion group in
Kansas. It's not ethnic Americanism.

*Dr. Bryant:* That's a nice clarification. But when I look at the
"New World"* publication and when I read the papers here,
that's not the impression that I get. I get a very different impression from them.

*Jonathan Wells:* What impression do you get?

*Dr. Bryant:* I get the impression that America is a chosen nation, singled out in the divine economy for a great role, and that its
whole history is, in a sense, moving toward the accomplishment of
this final role. And in terms of the newspaper** you know exactly
who the black hats are and who the white hats are. The newspaper
is not talking about a spiritual thing, or a potentiality; they're talking about decisions, very concrete decisions about who's going to
have this particular office, or who's going to be appointed to this
department in the national government in Washington, D.C.

*Lloyd Eby:* I think it's fair for you to be picking that up.
However, what I'd like to suggest is that the ideological positions
of the Church are not clear. What comes through in the newspaper
is some members' interpretations of what America's role is to be,
which is not necessarily rooted in Rev. Moon's thinking or theology. I'm often uncomfortable with the newspaper's opinions, and
others are too.

*Farley Jones:* I think you're right, and I think also that once
one sees the Unification Church as a dynamic and developing
group, and not a static one, then that problem gets solved over
time.

*Dr. Bryant:* I want to make one other historical analogy. It's
interesting to me to think about the Unification Church in relation

---

*The reference is to a bicentennial publication, "Toward Our Third Century," a *New
World* magazine published at the Unification Theological Seminary, Barrytown, New
York, July 4, 1976.

**The reference is to the daily newspaper published in New York City, *The News World.*

to the theocratic tradition of early America. That tradition founders, you know, on the problem of offspring. The Half-Way Covenant is the device in New England to get the children in, to make them saints. Now you have a solution for that problem that's unbelievable. You're going to give birth to these saints.

*Dr. Richardson:* Somehow we tend to focus on America and keep treating the Unification Church as an American millennial movement. Well, that's okay, because we're here in America. But the movement didn't even originate here. Do the leaders in Germany, for example, talk about what Germany can do for the sake of the Kingdom of Heaven on earth?

*Klaus Lindner:* Yes, I think they do.

*Tom Selover:* Here in America, there's a polemic to get America to do something. But that doesn't mean that the Church identifies the whole dispensation with America.

*Dr. Richardson:* That's interesting. What is the Church doing in Canada? This would be an interesting question for us to ask. My impression is that they do other things besides sell ginseng tea. (laughter) In Canada they're getting into the Quebec question, the question of the unity of Canada, which is interesting. They're organizing major conferences on this, and trying to promote the unity of Canada. They're not so much promoting the unity of Canada as a political union, but promoting the meeting of people from Quebec and the other provinces to discuss the question of the meaning of Canada.

But I think another thing that ought to be clear is that everybody in the Unification movement is anti-Communist. It's very important to get that out. When the faculty from the Seminary talked with Rev. Moon, he stated that the three things most on his mind were: first, the restoration of the family; second, the unification of Christianity and all religions; and third, the struggle against Communism. However, the struggle is not moralistic; it's dialectical. Farley Jones has made the point that the notion of the struggle against Communism is dialectical. That is, you don't just oppose Communism because you support capitalism. Unification opposes capitalistic individualism as much as it opposes Communism. So the effort is to oppose Communism in a dialectical way; that is, to incorporate its critique of capitalism while also overcoming its materialism, its anti-God bias. But it certainly is the case that in this dialectical sense, the struggle against Communism is part of the Unification theology and is non-negotiable.

*Klaus Lindner:* I think that this is how I saw the importance of America. Just before I joined the Church, I had been drafted into the army in Germany. I went to Reserve Officers Training and it convinced me completely that there was no way that Europe would resist Communism. Then I went to the university and the young Communists were the only ones who offered something that the young people could really identify with. And the only people who did something about capitalism were the young Communists. The churches were quiet. Already, at that time, I, personally, believed that the only thing that could keep Europe from being taken over quickly was its relationship to America. I felt that relationship was very important before I joined the Church. The whole Western world is very united, but America is most essential. When I came to America, I was actually quite disappointed that most Americans don't realize, or don't want to deal with, the fact that America is so important for so many countries. That's the political aspect of the whole "chosen" idea. America is the only country that has the heart to keep the freedom which the Western world has achieved.

*Dr. Bryant:* It seems to me that we must distinguish between two things here. One is a kind of strategic argument, an argument about America's place in the balance of power. On that level, we could have a discussion about America's role in relation to the Communists, and that doesn't bother me so much. The second thing is a theological argument concerning the status of worldly movements in the divine economy. What bothers me is that here I get the impression from some people that Communism is demonized. I don't know if you would use this term, but it seems to me that you understand Communism as the anti-Christ. And yet, when I talk to some of the people here, they seem to recognize the thing that was mentioned in talking about Germany: that is, that it is the young Communists who seem to embody a spirit of urgency in dealing with social and political problems. You seem to respect and admire that. Can you incorporate something into your thinking so that you could make this differentiation more sharply? Could you, for example, think about the Marxist tradition as a heretical Christian tradition, rather than as a satanic force?

*Lloyd Eby:* That's interesting. I think that I agree with you.

*Dr. Bryant:* About what? (laughter)

*Lloyd Eby:* I would be willing to accept that Marxism is a heretical Christian sect. Yet I think one also has to recognize that there's a difference between a distinction made for philosophical or evaluative purposes and the reality of the larger political situation. For example, it's very easy for us here in America to make distinctions like this. If you're, say, in South Korea or in Cambodia, where the reality is much more present, then that kind of distinction doesn't particularly help.

*Dr. Sawatsky:* Let me pick up this particular point. Darrol and I have a colleague who is from South Korea. He's a Presbyterian theologian. He has spoken out strongly against the present regime in South Korea. Now, he is not alone in this, as we all know. There are many like him. And the problem then arises. It's difficult for some of us who have just come through the Vietnam situation to be able to see righteousness in Park, just as we couldn't see it in Kee. And then to see Korea as the new Israel! Wow! That's impossible!

*Lynn Kim:* We're not saying Korea is God's example to the world.

*Lloyd Eby:* The fact is that South Korea is far from what any of us would like. But it has become that way, I think at least partially, through defending itself against North Korea. Even *Time* magazine last year compared South and North Korea and ended up comparing Park with Thomas Jefferson. *Time* magazine did this and *Time* doesn't like President Park at all. I think the fact remains that your friend is *persona non grata.* I don't condone that in the least; I don't agree with that approach. I think he should be allowed to say whatever he wants to. But the fact remains that if he were in North Korea, he wouldn't be *persona non grata,* he'd be dead.

*Lynn Kim:* Many Christians who were left in Korea in the 1950's were a remnant of those left after tremendous persecution by the Japanese, and also by North Korea. The Christians suffered tremendous persecution and executions under both regimes. To say you were Christian during the Japanese occupation was a very touchy business. In the park, close to where I lived in Korea, there were brass murals depicting a situation in which all the Christian leaders had been called to a meeting and then the doors were sealed and the church burned, and if anyone tried to jump out the window they were shot. So you had to choose to be a Christian in Korea. It wasn't an easy thing as it is here in New York.

*Linda Mitchell:* Let's think again about the word "chosen." I think that over and over in the Bible it says that God praised this nation not because they were a nation, but because of the faithful. It wasn't the nation as a whole. Sometimes God was able to forgive the nation on the merit of just a very, very few. So I think that God's grace is abundant everywhere you look. None of us deserve anything, least of all America or Korea. But I think that on the merit of a few people who sincerely want to see God's will fulfilled,

God can make use of those in that nation or in that family to bring life forth.

*Dr. Sawatsky:* How important is it that you have any nation identified this way or seen as this instrument? How important is that in the whole theology?

*Linda Mitchell:* I think it's important because you have to start somewhere.

*Dr. Bryant:* But the Kingdom of God — what does that have to do with one nation over against another, or one race over against another, or one class over against another? Isn't the Kingdom spiritual and universal? Can it be identified with these relative historical matters?

*Dr. Richardson:* Let's think about it this way for a minute. This is what Reformed theology would say. The issue is not whether God chooses one nation and not others. It's at a more abstract level. The question is: does God choose to work with national structures? I think that Unification doctrine is not that God chose America. God chooses every nation for some specific task. So God chooses in the present age, at least, to work with national structures. The national structure of Canada, the national structure of the United States, the national structure of Germany, etc. That's the point that needs to be made when somebody says, "God has a will for America." Americans think that God has a will for America and not for other nations. God choosing to work with America is like God choosing to work with every nation and to work with national structures, and then with international structures, just as He works with family and church structures. That's what gives Unification theology its political thrust. Instead of God relating Himself only to the souls of people, or just through the sacraments or through preaching, God is going to relate Himself to people through the whole range of institutional structures. Now, that's the key idea and, in a sense, that's one point that's so radical for individualistic Protestants as well as for sacramentalist Catholicism. It is not radical for the Reform tradition. The other point I'd like to argue is really this: interestingly, the criticism of the Unification Church in the United States is not that they're anti-Communist, but that they're anti-capitalist. That is, our children go off, give up their careers, don't become lawyers, work for nothing, and become part of these great big communes. So one has to ask: what is the Christian understanding of what is going on in the world?

*Dr. Sawatsky:* The criticism is that Rev. Moon is a capitalist. The criticism is that Unification is a church that seems to be wanting to bring the Kingdom of God in the economic realm. And that's offensive to many.

*Dr. Richardson:* Well, on that point, I think we understand many reasons why the Unification Church is in a sense not a Church, if by Church is meant the structure of church as it grew up in the church-state world. The Unification Church is a movement which is attempting to make God's will for the restoration of creation manifest in every sphere of life. And so, if you want to say it this way, it's like Communism as a movement. That is, it's a total ideology. In what sense is the Unification Church, or the Unification movement anti-Communist? It's anti-Communist in the sense that it's trying to attack the same problems that Communists are trying to attack by providing an alternative social philosophy: one which is critical of capitalism, private profit, individualism, and a number of other things.

*Dr. Sawatsky:* But there's a question here. What is the vision of the new economy?

*Lokesh Mazumdar:* I'd like to point out something. So far our discussion seems to be restricted to the socio-economic and political level, as if that's all there is to it. Rev. Moon never operates on that level without always including the vast and unexplored spiritual level. The Communists are very efficient in doing a lot of things. As far as a country like India is concerned, where there is extensive poverty, the Communists can perhaps improve the economic situation. But because of their lack of a doctrine of the spirit world and the afterlife, anything that they would have to offer would be horribly limited. When you reach the economic ceiling, where do you go from there? The thing that constantly comes out of all the masters that I've ever heard, and from the *Divine Principle,* is that the Kingdom of Heaven has to be everlasting. No matter how high a civilization is, if it has holes that would allow it to crumble and fall, you cannot found the Kingdom. That disqualifies every single nation that exists and all ideologies and all economic systems and all political systems and everything else.

*Dr. Bryant:* I'm very happy to hear you say that.

*Dr. Sawatsky:* There's one thing I want to pick up here, and that is the comparison that was made between Unification and Communism. The notion that Unification is a movement, and not a Church, is very important. It seems to me that a characteristic of American religion, especially since separation of church and state, has been a move to two polarities: one individual and one national. The church, as the primary vehicle of the Kingdom, has disappeared in favor of the nation as the agent. Now, I think we're catching the same thing here. It is not the Church which brings in the new order, but rather a nation or group of nations which brings in the new order. That is a particular Americanization of theology which is very interesting: that the Kingdom is coming through nation-states, that nation-states are important entities in themselves, that national borders which are due to the accidents of history, are, however, not accidents of history, but are of ultimate import because they are the part of the economy of the ultimate will of God.

*Lokesh Mazumdar:* Situationally speaking, I think that's true. But when we go back to the creation, then we can see that there was no nation. Adam and Eve weren't created in one single nation. We can't really overlook that in our journeying toward the Kingdom of Heaven. One has to remember that in the end, there will be one family of man under God. Now, whether we live as a people confined to the earth, or live as a people confined to three continents of the earth, or whether we live as a people in twenty solar systems, doesn't really matter. What matters is that all people will be a family, and that that family would have as its center the presence of God.

*Dr. Richardson:* I want to explain this. Rod, I think you're right on this point: that the nation has, within Unification theology, a permanent significance. But this is not to say that it has ultimate significance. Now, as I hear it said over and over again, the important things are God-centered individuals, God-centered families, God-centered nations, God-centered world. There's a hierarchy in the way they are related to one another: first, the centering of your life in God as an individual, *then* creating God-centered families, uniting your families in a nation, *then* in the international order. Also I think that what must be said is that the international community, which is an international community of nations, is international, not non-national. The international community is a higher value than the nation. But you have to be committed to your nation. You come into the international community as an American or as a Canadian. It seems to me that it's only those people who don't firmly believe in the international community and international citizenship who would say that Unification is fundamentally a nationalistic group. It seems to me that the whole structure of the movement is to say that the nation is important as the precondition for membership in the international community. The reason why I think that that message is not heard in America is because Americans don't really believe in an international community. We don't learn foreign languages, so what it means to be part of an international community is not a reality for Americans.

*Dr. Bryant:* The question still remains. It is a problem of the relationship of the American nation to other nations. Why, for example, isn't the destiny of the international world dependent upon Chile, Cuba and the Soviet Union instead of the United States, Britain and the Northern European Alliance?

*Lokesh Mazumdar:* Theoretically, it could very well be, but I don't see that as the case right now.

*Dr. Bryant:* Do you mean it's accidental? It seems that America has a special destiny which is grounded in divine providence.

*Jonathan Wells:* You don't seem to believe that God works in this way: choosing one individual or two. Yet, if we are to believe the Bible, that's exactly how God does work and always has worked, starting with Cain and Abel, Jacob and Esau. There's really no good reason why God should choose Jacob before he was even born, and yet He did. And it wasn't because Esau was evil. The *Divine Principle* teaches that what God began in individuals, in Adam's family, in Cain and Abel, and later, in Jacob and Esau, has, as the world's population expanded and providence grew, gradually grown into nations. Nations are the new units that God deals with.

*Dr. Bryant:* Let me interject here. The Cain/Abel antithesis, it seems to me, is one that runs *through* the heart of every man and every community. The antithesis is not one community over against another, one class over against another, one nation over against another.

*Lynn Kim:* That's the whole point.

*Dr. Bryant:* No, it's not the point! How can you agree? You see the Cain/Abel typology as a way to distinguish individuals and groups and nations *from* one another. I mean you *are* saying something about the dependence of the entire historical order upon the destiny of America. Now, however much you want to qualify it, you can't get away from it.

*Dr. Richardson:* Look, I don't understand what you're saying. Let's look at it this way: in the heart of every individual there is the struggle between the flesh and spirit. Every individual lives in sin. There's no question about that. Now, in Scripture, it's quite clear that even though people are born in sin and live in sin, it's yet the case that God does choose and use individuals and nations. The category of chosenness relates to the providence of God. In Scripture, Cyrus is used in the providence of God.

*Dr. Bryant:* I'm not sure that that helps.

*Dr. Sawatsky:* Besides, that's in the Old Testament, where this difference still is represented as the difference between one nation as opposed to another. But that's no longer the case. In the New Testament it's put on a different level, a universal level.

*Dr. Richardson:* What is the difference now?

*Dr. Sawatsky:* The difference is not between Israel and non-Israel. The difference is now between the forces of unrighteousness and the forces of righteousness. That difference doesn't break down along national lines.

*Lloyd Eby:* There's a sense in which Unification is beyond the New Testament or, if you want to say it in a different way, there's a sense in which Unificationism goes back, takes up the Old Testament, and continues where it should have been taken up.

*Lokesh Mazumdar:* May I interject here and remind you that we should not get stuck on the international and worldwide level. There's a cosmic level beyond that. I think it's wholesome to remember that.

*Dr. Bryant:* Lokesh keeps reminding us of these spirits and the spiritual world. Is that something you really want us to talk about?

*Lokesh Mazumdar:* The cosmic level is more important. We only have sixty years upon the earth.

*Dr. Bryant:* Thus far everyone is saying that the great point of our discussion is really these sixty years. Now you're saying that doesn't mean as much to you as the stuff that comes after. (laughter)

*Lokesh Mazumdar:* That's *the* major difference between Communism and Unificationism. That's the most important difference. The Communists would focus their sight on sixty years and seek to solve all the problems that they encounter in that span of sixty years. We won't do the same thing. We won't use guns and bullets to solve every problem in sixty years because we have the conviction that there's ample time. There's plenty of opportunity beyond this life to solve those problems. We believe that in our life of faith and in this journey toward establishing or building the Kingdom of Heaven on earth and going to where we would like to be, there's a connection between the spirit world and the physical world. In other words, a person may be helped along the way by his ancestors or by some other spirits, like Jesus or Abraham. There's a very conscious effort on the part of the Unification Church to make the proper conditions so that this happens.

*Dr. Klaaren:* But even for the spirit world, from my talk with Janine, it's clear that the physical world is absolutely essential. So you do have a lot to do in these sixty years.

*Tom Selover:* That's why we're talking about this. There would be no reason for us to be here if that wasn't so.

*Jonathan Wells:* We talked about the creation and the Fall, and now we're actually talking about the restoration. And it started with Cain and Abel. Adam and Eve fell, they weren't at all repentant, God was left with this mess, and somehow He had to try to start the restoration. So He had Cain and Abel to choose from, or I should say to use, and how was He going to do that? Well, *Divine Principle* teaches that He chose Abel for various reasons. I won't try to explain it because it's a little complicated, but it was not necessarily because Abel was better. But when He chose Abel, Cain was angry and jealous. God arranged it so that both Cain and Abel had to overcome their fallen nature in order to solve their own dispute. Abel had to overcome his arrogance. His arrogance stemmed from the fact that God preferred him. So his fallen nature expressed itself as arrogance, just as my fallen nature expresses itself as arrogance in the same situation. And Cain's fallen nature expressed itself as envy, as jealousy. And the fact was that neither of the two of them was able to overcome. As the *Divine Principle* teaches, Abel stayed arrogant, and Cain stayed jealous and killed him. And so the restoration failed. This strategy of God has been multiplied through human history on the individual level, family level and the national level. This is what we are getting at when we talk about politics: the strategy of restoration.

If you stand back from the situation, regardless of how anti-American you may be (and several of us in the Church are anti-American, or were), the fact is, I think, that God has chosen America, even if we don't like it. I think it's easy to see the Soviet Union, for example, in a Cain position. Now, Abel can become arrogant and blow it again, which is, it seems to me, what America is doing.

*Dr. Bryant:* Jonathan, do you feel that God has also chosen Chile?

*Jonathan Wells:* Yes.

*Dr. Bryant:* Do you feel you have an obligation to learn what that means in the same detail that you feel you need to understand what it means to say that God has chosen America?

*Jonathan Wells:* By Chile, you're saying every other country?

*Dr. Bryant:* No I meant what I said.

*Jonathan Wells:* Just Chile?

*Dr. Bryant:* Yes.

*Jonathan Wells:* Well, my own personal responsibility is to know what my position is in God's providence, and if I'm in a

Cain-Abel situation. Then I have to know who my Abel or who my Cain is, and understand how I can restore the situation. And if I happen to be an American, and if Soviet Russia is Cain on a national level then that's the situation I have to understand. Now, if I'm a Cuban, a Chilean Marxist, or a Chilean Christian or Fascist, or whatever else, then I have to understand my position in Chile or in Peru or whatever. But what I'm talking about now is my position as it really is. I think it has international implications clearly. I don't think that can be denied.

*Dr. Richardson:* Let's ask about some other cases. What, for example, would they say about Germany? Is Germany, as a nation, placed within the providence of God? We have two Germans here, so we can ask them. We can put it to anybody from another nation. What do Christa or Klaus say about Germany?

*Klaus Lindner:* Germany is, in Europe, in a very similar situation to, for example, Korea. Germany is divided into East and West. The Unification Church in Germany is working very hard to have the people in Germany develop a consciousness of all of Europe. Western Europe has to find some unity. And also, the Unification Church is working against Communism. Germany, France and England have very important roles in the unity of Europe.

*Rev. Calitis:* Do you two want unity among those nations? What do you two want?

*Klaus Lindner:* Ideologically? Unity in relation to Communism.

*Christa Dabeck:* To bring the German people to the consciousness of the danger of Communism. There's much wishy-washy opinion over there. People are not sure whether it is better to live in a democratic country or in a Communist country. They're not clear what Communism really means. Unification is working very hard to give people a clear understanding about this.

God is working today to bring His Kingdom on earth. That is what we teach. God is trying to work in a special way at this time in history to bring His Kingdom. He is being opposed right now in His work of salvation, in His work of bringing a God-centered Kingdom on earth, by a basically atheistic system which says it is bringing a secular kingdom on earth. If Communism takes over the world, it'll be very difficult to establish a God-centered Kingdom on earth. So one of our first steps is to keep the whole world from becoming Communist, because we'll then have a very difficult time in our evangelical work. So that's the first step. That's why we are anti-Communist, that's why nations can't help but get involved. God's problem in the beginning was one man and one woman who fell. Then they multiplied and there was a fallen family. Then there was a fallen tribe, and then there was a fallen nation. Now we've got these big nations that are trying to take over the world. So, somehow, they have to be stopped.

*Dr. Sawatsky:* The reason why this is such an important matter to you, I take it, is that you see that God's providence cannot override human freedom. Is that right? That's why it's such a problem. You see that Jesus' mission finally failed because there wasn't the human response that there should have been. Then conceivably, if Communism were to be successful, God would be vanquished.

*Jonathan Wells:* God Himself is not vanquished, but His people are going to have a heck of a time for a long time if Communism is successful. Communism is not created by God, so it will collapse eventually. But let's keep it from taking over the whole world and having to collapse internally and having God start all over again.

*Dr. Richardson:* I'd like to make a general comment about this whole discussion. One thing I have noticed is that when we speak about these political things, the Jewish people have very little problem understanding. It does cause a problem for Christians, in particular for Protestant Christians in America, because the Protestant Christian conception of the godly Kingdom is wholly spiritualized.

*Lloyd Eby:* That's one reason. I think there's another reason, too. That is, Protestant Christianity in general does not have a conception of the Kingdom of God as a renewal or restoration of the physical world, which includes all the institutions that one sees in the world. Now, it's interesting that we started out talking about the restoration of man to God and the spiritual restoration. Protestant Christianity has no problem with spiritual restoration. When we go on to talk about the family, to the restoration of the Second Blessing, to some extent Christianity can follow that, to some extent it can't. Christianity is partly comfortable with that and partly uncomfortable. And when we go on to talk about what we would call the Third Blessing, that is, the restoration of the physical world into the Kingdom of Heaven, that's always the time when problems come out. We start getting into problems about politics, economics, those things. That's where the most difficulty comes for Christians in accepting Unificationism. I think the reason for that difficulty is that Christianity has never had a foundation for appreciating what we would call the Third Blessing. It has no general foundation because Jesus was crucified and there-

fore salvation in Christianity becomes a spiritual thing, a matter of
two Kingdoms. Hence Christianity can't really talk very well about
such things as education, politics and economics. It has never been
able to solve any of those problems.

*Dr. Vander Goot:* You're just simply wrong.

*Dr. Richardson:* I'd like to make a suggestion here. This
morning we played "Christian theologians reply to Unification
doctrine," and we talked about the doctrine of Creation, Christology, on and on. Now why don't we just tell the Unification people what the right Christian social theory is? Let's tell them where
they're wrong in their view of the Kingdom of God on earth. Now
I'm going to begin by telling you. (laughter)

*Dr. Bryant:* My problem is I don't really think that what
you're saying is right, Lloyd. The problem is, as I understand Augustine, that the role of nations in the divine economy is something
we don't know. That would be my position, too. I don't know. I'll
be very straight about that. I don't know what the role of the nations is in the divine economy. I do believe that there is some role,
but I don't know what it is. You see, what's operating here is simply the Protestant principle of criticism. I do know historically
about different kinds of dangers, certain kinds of difficulty, certain kinds of problems. But no, I don't know what the "right
Christian social theory" is. I'm willing to leave it at a fairly theoretical level because I don't have anything beyond that to say.

*Dr. Richardson:* Wouldn't you say that if you go to, for example, the National Council of Churches and ask them you'll get
two answers; there are only two answers in the Christian Church.
There are the people who are spiritualizers: two-kingdom people
who are Augustinians. Their answer is: "We don't know." Right?
And you get the modified view of the Catholics, who say, "Well,
we don't know, but any state that will let us celebrate Mass and
have Church schools is okay." Right? You get different kinds of
spiritualizers, and the other group you get are the Christian Marxists. Now, what I find interesting is that most of us who belong to
the East Coast Liberal establishment can live comfortably with the
Christian Marxists. All the big names are Christian Marxists:
Moltmann, Metz, Alves. We listen to the people who are Christian
Marxists, right? Yet for the Unification people it's really *Christian*
Marxism, whereas for people like Moltmann, it's Marxism with a
little bit of God around the outside. Really, there's no attempt to
work Christian material into the Marxist theory. But we have a lot
of appreciation for Marxism, and I think that we could even say
that it's almost an orthodox way for a Christian theologian today

to build a social philosophy: namely, to take Marxism on. If you go to the World Council of Churches, you'll find that they tend fundamentally to be Christian Marxists.

It seems to me that insofar as there would be any critique of what Unification says, it tends to be a critique that comes out of the spiritualizing of the pre-Marxist period: namely, we don't know the function of providence, God is hidden, there are two kingdoms, and we know how dangerous millennialism is. That seems to be a reasonable position. But can we criticize Unification's political enthusiasm unless we have something else to offer?

*Dr. Bryant:* I am not criticizing their political enthusiasm; I'm criticizing their theological formulations. I agree that we need a Christian social theory and I'm glad that the Unification Church is working on one, but that doesn't mean that we can't engage in critical conversation about their position.

*Lynn Kim:* I think that in our discussions we, as Unification Church members, had to be vague this afternoon in speaking of the national level because our movement is not on a national level. Our American movement is still primarily on an individual level, cracking into the family level, and just touching a societal level. We have a Church and we have believers, but we're nowhere near approaching any kind of national instrument. So how can we talk about how God is going to work on the national level? We aren't there yet. But if we can awaken the conscience of America to begin to serve the world, this would be the beginning.

# PRACTICE, STYLE AND AUTHORITY
# IN THE UNIFICATION MOVEMENT

*Dr. Bryant:* I thought we might get more details about the style of life within the Unification movement.

*Dr. Sawatsky:* The one thing you haven't told us much about is the crash course that starts the program. Tell us the basic content, and who does the teaching. Especially the content. Is there a standard content?

*Jonathan Wells:* We use the *Study Guide* for the *Divine Principle* as a guide for our lectures. The *Divine Principle* is condensed and presented more systematically in the *Study Guide.* The *Study Guide* is much easier to read than the Black Book, I think.

*Diana Muxworthy:* Did you want a picture of what the workshop itself is like?

*Dr. Sawatsky:* Yes. I want to see what this formation is all about.

*Diana Muxworthy:* We begin with a personal one-to-one discussion of the *Divine Principle.* After that you go to a three-day workshop; from a three-day, if you wish, you go on to a seven-day workshop; if you wish, you can then go on to a twenty-one-day workshop; if you wish, you can then go on to a forty-day, and finally we have a 120-day workshop, which is actually a preparation for missionary work. The three-day workshops are the beginning. On the East coast, they usually begin on Friday night. It's different out West. I'm not familiar with their schedule.

In general, people arrive on Friday night and simply talk, and then sleep. We usually wake up about six-thirty and have exercises, a prayer or worship service, breakfast, and then we begin the first lecture which concerns the Principle of Creation. And then people are divided into small teams with a group leader to reflect on the *Divine Principle.* There's a break around three in the afternoon or so for sports. We play soccer and other games, depending on the season. The central concern is an understanding of the *Divine Principle* which includes living it also. Then, there are usually more *Divine Principle* lectures. Sometimes, instead of lectures on the *Divine Principle,* there's a talk on prayer, or a talk on parental fears or personal testimonies. Usually it ends pretty late. That's what the media picks up on. Midnight is the cutoff point, but usually so much is going on in the group that it's difficult to get people to sleep. Usually about one or two, things quiet down. We follow the same schedule until Sunday. But that varies, too. Sometimes it goes until Monday, depending on how much of the lecture still needs to be given.

*Jonathan Wells:* My experience teaching at a workshop has always been that I had to force people to go to bed. Everybody wants to stay up and talk all night, so we have to insist that they go to bed. I think that over the past two years we've been experimenting a lot with our training programs. The program Diana explained was evolved around November of 1974 when we began expanding from the three- to seven- to twenty-one-, forty- and 120-day workshops. We followed that program for about a year, maybe even better than a year and a half. Since about March of 1976, we haven't had the forty- and the 120-day training sessions.

*Klaus Lindner:* A very small percentage of the members went through the forty-day session. The structure itself is very flexible to allow for the needs of many different people.

*Linda Mitchell:* Yes. It is only recently that a program has been worked out. When I heard the Principle, there was no such thing as a workshop. There was a Center in our town run by two people. My brother and I would go over there and one night they would teach us part of the Principle of Creation, and then another night we'd just talk. It wasn't structured at all. I never had a three-day, seven-day or twenty-one-day workshop. I never had any kind of formal instruction.

*Klaus Lindner:* When I was in Germany, the initial training was very much centered around reading and discussing the *Divine Principle.* Not many people had very much teaching experience. They just read the book together or read it at home. Most of the book I read at home. Then I decided to join. That's quite a common experience for members in Europe.

*Jonathan Wells:* I joined in West Virginia, and I was a member for three months before I went to my first workshop.

*Lynn Kim:* I was a member for a year and a half before the first workshop ever took place. The person who taught me had to read me the book. He didn't know how to lecture. I don't know why he wanted to read it to me. I guess he thought the spirit would come through better if he read it; but I knew I could read faster, so it irritated me. (laughter)

*Lokesh Mazumdar:* In addition to the regular *Divine Principle* presentation there is a series of lectures called the Internal Guidance. The idea of Internal Guidance is to give an internal experience to the person. This way they would have a deeper experiential understanding of certain expressions in the *Divine Principle,* such as foundation of faith, and foundation of substance. Some people had a very good experience with that, and some people didn't. These lectures aren't in the Black Book. They are generally about God and his relation to personal experience.

*Dr. Sawatsky:* Is that still being used?

*Lokesh Mazumdar:* I don't know if it's being used right now.

*Janine Anderson:* Prayer is also very important in coming to understand God and our beliefs.

*Dr. Sawatsky:* Is there any guidance for your piety in written form or formalized in some fashion? I was asking yesterday about prayer books and hymn books, but what I mean now is a guide to piety.

*Lynn Kim:* Well, not really.

*Klaus Lindner:* Internal Guidance is a guide to a way of life.

*Lynn Kim:* Internal Guidance is just one person's experience with God.

*Lokesh Mazumdar:* The whole purpose of the workshop is to give the person an experience with God and to deepen his understanding. We also try, if possible, to give the person some sense of the role of Rev. Moon as the central figure of the whole movement and the channel for God, and we encourage him to develop some kind of a relationship with the other participants as brothers and sisters. But it doesn't always work out that way.

*Dr. Sawatsky:* It seems to me that these training sessions must be very, very important, though. When you come here to the Seminary you are bombarded by people from all kinds of other backgrounds: Calvinists, Catholics, Jews, and so forth. Yet there doesn't seem to be any shaking of the foundations for you. You seem to take it all, and yet maintain quite comfortably your own perception of what truth is. Someplace you must have come to a very solid sense of what you believe. That must happen in these training sessions.

*Lloyd Eby:* Well, it's partly from the training sessions, but more important is the common faith that we have, and the living of that faith every day. I think the ability for us here in the Seminary to be exposed to almost any tradition, to engage in creative dialogue and to question and explore, bespeaks a very strong faith on which we stand.

*Dr. Sawatsky:* But it must be more than simply heartfelt faith. That faith must be well worked out intellectually, because the ability of you all to engage in conversation has been I think, rather unusual. There is a deviation from one person to the next, but it's deviation within a common framework.

*Lynn Kim:* I think you have to remember that most of us have been exposed to some extent to these other traditions and influences before. Many of us shopped around, looking for a meaningful belief that could absorb us. We chose Unification over everything else, but we're still open to investigating other ways.

*Joe Stenson:* There's a kind of solidness in relationship to the *Divine Principle* throughout our movement. Also, there's a kind of facility with language that we have gained because most of the things we do are very outgoing. For example, the twenty-one-day workshop includes seven days of lecture, seven days of fundraising, seven days of witnessing. You really find things out in talking with people. Most members are constantly talking with people about what we believe and what we think. The experience of fundraising is very much like that, too. It's very much of a spiritual discipline.

*Diana Muxworthy:* Fundraising was a powerful experience for me. I was out on my own and I had to make a decision: do I believe in the *Divine Principle* and am I willing to go through this? To me, fundraising was a very spiritual experience in that it reaffirmed my faith. Every day I had to question what I believed.

*Jonathan Wells:* The 120-day training session that used to be taught here in Barrytown consisted of sixty days of lectures and discussion, then three weeks of fundraising and forty days of pioneering. For pioneering, they took us out with our equipment, including a portable blackboard and a bicycle, and left us somewhere. I got dropped in Stamford, Connecticut on a Sunday afternoon with twenty dollars in my pocket and instructions to set up a Center. So I just started from scratch. I slept out in a Lord and Taylor parking lot (laughter) and started from there. I was the only Church member in a town of 100,000 people. We are doing this all over New England. Later that summer and fall it was done all over the country. I'd say that most of the Principle that I know, I learned that way. (laughter)

*Dr. Sawatsky:* I think probably all of us that are teachers know that one of the best ways to learn anything is to have to teach it.

*Lynn Kim:* From the minute you know something you start teaching it. If you've heard one chapter, you go and teach it to someone. I was surprised to discover that on the sixth day of the seven-day workshop, they took people up to Albany and started them witnessing. Some went out in trepidation, and some of them were really eager. But it was a tremendous experience for all of them. They felt such joy and came back alive and bright and talking a mile a minute. You get into really good discussions, really practical. Your knowledge comes from your need to explain it to someone else.

*Diana Muxworthy:* Something that has really helped me is understanding that the purpose of the Church is not to become another denomination. The purpose of the Unification Church is to revitalize churches, to bring Christianity alive, to understand all world religions and to become a part of all of them rather than to become separate from all of them. So I've never felt that I'm against anyone. I really want to understand other people rather than fight them. I really want to understand them and help them and help myself, and together go towards God's world.

*Dr. Bryant:* Sometimes I am a bit uncomfortable using the word "Unification Church" since your official title is "The Holy Spirit Association for the Unification of World Christianity." Do you feel any uneasiness about using the term "Church," or does it signify some kind of change or development within Unification?

*Farley Jones:* I'd like to say just one thing about that. In the early 1960's we were known as the Unified Family. And in 1970, our charter of incorporation in the state of California specified three possible names for the organization: the Holy Spirit Association for the Unification of World Christianity, the Unified Family and the Unification Church. We'd always been using the Unified Family. But in the 1970's we felt that so long as we kept the name Unified Family, we'd be generally perceived as a flower-children type group. In an effort to be perceived in relation to the Christian tradition we began to call ourselves the Unification Church.

*Lynn Kim:* Most of us around at that time really groaned and grumbled under the Church name because it made it difficult to witness to people our own age, mostly young college age people. We'd say "Church" and they'd say "blaah!" It was really tough.

*Lokesh Mazumdar:* I think that at that time the presentation of the *Divine Principle* was not so Biblically-oriented. It was simply the general Principle, the Principle of Creation. After 1970, it was much more Biblically-oriented.

*Dr. Sawatsky:* Do you mind explaining why that occurred?

*Lokesh Mazumdar:* I think it was just an expansion of the Christian foundation of the *Divine Principle.*

*Klaus Lindner:* Also, I think that the *Divine Principle* was not yet translated in the form that it is right now. And also, Rev. Moon was not yet here in America.

*Lynn Kim:* It was also due to the greater influence of the Korean movement. The missionaries had come, but left here, and had done whatever they could. Then Rev. Moon's presence brought the tradition of the Church as it had developed in Korea and Japan.

*Dr. Sawatsky:* That was more Christian than the early Church teaching in America?

*Lynn Kim:* Yes.

*Linda Mitchell:* In Italy, I don't think it is called a church. Do you know what the name of it is, Janine?

*Janine Anderson:* I think it's called an association in Italy, and also in France.

*Klaus Lindner:* It might be changed in Germany, but when I was there it was the Holy Spirit Association.

*Lynn Kim:* I personally feel very uncomfortable saying I'm from an association. (laughter) In Korean the word "church" doesn't have the same limitations as our word "church" does. It can be a church, it can be an association, it can be a group of people assembled for a purpose. It does happen to be the word that they've selected to use for the Protestant churches, but it's a flexible word in Korean.

*Lloyd Eby:* I think, too, that the relationship between the Unification movement and the Christian churches is a dynamic thing. It goes through many phases. We would never want it to be a separate organization. But it's one way to start being recognized as a member of the community of churches. But that's not, as you have gathered, the goal we want to reach. Now we're beginning to de-emphasize Unification Churchiness and to talk about an interdenominational, interfaith type of thing.

*Lokesh Mazumdar:* There was an idea a long time ago that if the Unification Church wasn't able to bring about the unification of all the Christian denominations, then there would probably be the creation of an additional movement to bring the Unification Church and other Christian churches together. (laughter)

*Dr. Klaaren:* And if that didn't work, I suppose there would probably be one more church. (laughter)

*Dr. Bryant:* Could we turn this discussion to pick up the question of the place of Rev. Moon and the place of the *Divine Principle?* I'm still not clear about the place of the *Divine Principle* in relation to the Old and New Testament, or, for that matter, in relation to the sacred scriptures of other traditions. Is the *Divine Principle* a Third Testament? Is it a new systematic theology? Is it a new interpretation of the Christian scriptures?

*Lloyd Eby:* In my opinion, that question is difficult for us to answer. The relationships between the *Divine Principle* and the Christian Scriptures are dynamic. The question, I think, would suggest that there's a static answer to that question. I don't think we have that answer. In other words, I feel equally comfortable reading the Black Book or reading the *Study Guide* or reading copies of Rev. Moon's speeches, or reading the Old Testament, or reading the New Testament, or reading the Koran. I feel equally comfortable with any of these, and I use them all either as guides for spiritual life or guides for intellectual reflection. It certainly is the case that there is a kind of primacy to Rev. Moon's person, and to his words or to his speeches that I suppose we wouldn't give to the other writings. Let's put it this way. If there were a question which required us to give precedence to one source of truth over another, then we would probably give that precedence to Rev. Moon because he is a living being and can therefore give a particular response to a particular question in a particular context. He can be more specific than a written text. I suppose we would give second place to the Black Book version of the *Divine Principle* although I've heard some of our own members say that the Black Book has serious problems in the way it's written. I agree that there are problems with it.

*Dr. Bryant:* Okay. However, it seems to me that there must be — and maybe it's just a problem of articulation — some principle which allows you to say it doesn't matter whether you read the Koran, the Old Testament, or the New Testament. I can't quite believe that. You're not reading these texts as if they were texts that just happened to cross your table. Right? You read them in the light of some other truth.

*Lloyd Eby:* The principle behind our reading would be the conviction that truth is eternal and unchanging, and that throughout history one can find expressions of truth. There is truth in each one of the world religions. Although truth is eternal and unchanging, the process of revelation is an historical one. We believe that now, in the person and in the message of Rev. Moon, we have the fullest expression of truth. Yet, wherever one finds any kind of religious experience in the history of mankind, one will find at least some part of the content of that truth. We would see the divine principle as a principle underlying the whole process of creation and the whole process of human restoration. Everywhere, in creation and restoration, the divine principle is at work.

*Klaus Lindner:* I would say that it's true that we find the divine principle when we read the Bible and when we read the Koran. Therefore, we can read all texts confidently, because we have a basic principle. We learn more about the divine principle through reading in other religious traditions.

*Dr. Bryant:* Would it be wrong to say it this way: the divine principle is the revelation, and you see traces of that revelation in other religions, other traditions, other experiences?

*Lloyd Eby:* I wouldn't want to say it quite like that. I would say that the divine principle is a principle underlying the whole process of creation and the whole process of restoration of the universe and that one can see traces of that in every kind of revelation. So it's not a revelatory principle; it's a principle underlying the process of creation and the process of restoration throughout the universe. Wherever one sees expressions of that in any kind of revelation, one is seeing expressions of that principle.

*Dr. Bryant:* But is it not the case that you are building more definitely within the Christian context than you are within the Buddhist, or the Hindu?

*Lloyd Eby:* I think the answer to that is once again both/and. We have people in the Church who had no Christian background, but were Buddhist or Shinto; and yet their understanding and appreciation of the divine principle is at least as strong as that of people who come out of the Christian tradition. We would say that the reason we give a primacy to Christianity is because it is the closest expression of the Principle.

*Farley Jones:* I have a feeling that that statement shortchanges our perception of the role of the Judeo-Christian tradition in the *Divine Principle.*

*Lynn Kim:* And of Christ Himself. I think, Lloyd, that you misunderstand the teaching of the central providence and the crucial providence. The central providence of God throughout history and the only one in which He, Himself, has consistently invaded mankind's history is the Judeo-Christian tradition. You have Buddha saying, "I meditated and I understood"; or in another religion you have somebody saying, "I perceive that society works this way." That is not God invading history as He has in the Judeo-Christian tradition. The Judeo-Christian tradition is the history of God desperately trying to transform man.

*Joe Stenson:* I think we make a distinction between what we would term Adamic religion, or religion that comes in the line of Adam, which is as Lynn says the direct revelation of God to man, and an archangelic religion like Islam or Mormonism. In these latter, a revelation comes by way of an angel; but the Judeo-Christian tradition sees the central providence of God moving throughout history. The archangel religions are from a high realm of the spiritual world, and their knowledge of truth is very close to God's. But they're built around the side of that central providence perceived by the Judeo-Christian tradition.

*Dr. Sawatsky:* I heard you pray in the name of Jesus. You weren't praying in the name of Buddha. "When salvation comes, to Jesus I return," somebody said.

*Klaus Lindner:* The Christian tradition is something like a red thread in history through which restoration is to be accomplished. But other religious traditions also lead mankind in other parts of the world, to a level as high as they can reach. At the time salvation is being accomplished, the other people in the world should be on a spiritual level from which they also can understand what's happening. At the time of Jesus, for example, Israel certainly was prepared to understand Jesus; but the whole world, the Roman Empire, was prepared to spread the message, and the other religions prepared other parts of the world. We don't see Buddhism as against Judaism or Christianity, but as a preparation for understanding God's revelations through Judeo-Christianity.

*Tom Selover:* The *Divine Principle* says that in this time, a new understanding or a more completed understanding has to come in order to clarify the Bible and all religions.

*Dr. Sawatsky:* Are we speaking of the Last Days? These are the Last Days, right?

*Dr. Bryant:* Some of the things I've read, suggest it's not through the Judeo-Christian tradition, but through Rev. Moon, that we get the glasses, that we get the message decoded. The Bible is a coded message, right? Rev. Moon decodes it. It's his revelation.

*Lynn Kim:* That's the Last Days aspect. You remember, in the final days you will see clearly, though now you see darkly; and Jesus says, "I have many things to say to you, but I cannot say them now, you cannot bear them yet." Now those things are very clearly and easily opened. In the Last Days, we will not believe in God, but we will know God. He will be a real part of our lives.

*Lokesh Mazumdar:* One thing that's central is the role of Christ, the role of the Messiah. Most other religions have a central figure too, but that figure is usually the avatar or some sort of spiritual leader — one of many who have appeared consistently in different ages at different times when the need came. Now, Christianity was not meant to be Christian. Christianity was meant to be universal, just as Judaism was meant to be universal. But that never happened, and so, when we talk of Christianity today, we're talking about Christianity as it is, whereas in reality the value of Christianity should have been universal. This is where the role of the principal revelator, the role of Rev. Moon, the role of the central figure in this particular age who decodes this message, comes in.

*Lynn Kim:* But once you have that clear, the things that Lloyd said are perfectly true: you see the *Divine Principle* as describing the principles of the universe. Through it we can understand any religion, and see how it fits into the universal picture.

*Dr. Clark:* You people are in a very unique position in relationship to the other religions we've been talking about, because your oral tradition is still going on. You said before that Rev. Moon's voice itself is still the primary thing, even above and beyond the *Divine Principle.* When Rev. Moon dies are you going to have something like an apostolic succession for Church leadership? Will the person at the head of the movement retain Moon's position as the living voice of authority? Or will the Black Book become more central as a kind of text as happened with the Christians in the years after the first few centuries?

*Diana Muxworthy:* I think the *Divine Principle* can be considered as the theology of the Church. The tradition Rev. Moon is transmitting through his words and through his speeches places more emphasis on personal spiritual growth. His words aren't directed at changing the *Divine Principle* or saying anything different from the Black Book, but are concerned with relating the Principle to each individual in his life and in his struggles to attain a clear understanding of God. I think that his speeches will be used in the same fashion even after his death.

*Klaus Lindner:* Many of his speeches are directed to specific situations. The speeches don't actually change anything that's basic to the *Divine Principle.* They elaborate. Points become much clearer as more examples are used to illustrate them.

*Dr. Sawatsky:* Would it be possible for me to say that the *Divine Principle* is essentially right, that I believe in the notion of family, of world community, etc. as you do, but to say that I do not accept Moon as the Revelator, as the new Messiah?

*Jonathan Wells:* I'd like to answer that. I have a very difficult time separating Rev. Moon from the Principle. Not that they aren't separable, but the Principle is a theory, and in fact our Study Guide says it's like a scientific hypothesis. You test it the way you test a scientific hypothesis — by experience. If we had just the theory, it would be very interesting, but I doubt very seriously if we would have a movement. That's my personal opinion. The fact that Rev. Moon has managed to embody that Principle, for me, makes the movement. Now, if he were to part visibly from that Principle, so that he and the *Divine Principle* as we understand it were at odds with each other, I think the movement would fall apart.

*Dr. Clark:* If they parted, but not when he dies.

*Jonathan Wells:* That's right, not when he dies. But if he were to desert the Principle, I don't know what might happen. But the fact is, they are one. He is the embodiment of what he teaches in the Principle. Now, I can test the Principle independently of Rev. Moon. But when I see Rev. Moon fulfilling the direction of that Principle and showing me that a human being can do that, that really gives me hope.

*Dr. Sawatsky:* That's interesting. Now let's get straight what he's speaking about here. You start out by speaking of the Messiah. Is Rev. Moon the Messiah?

*Jonathan Wells:* Well, we talked about this yesterday. Some people say he is, some people say he will be, and some people say it's not even determined yet who is or who isn't. I don't find it necessary to think of him as the Messiah. I think of him as the champion of the Kingdom of God. My relationship with him is on many levels. But I can see him as the point of the spear that's opening the way.

*Dr. Sawatsky:* Do you relate to Rev. Moon in terms, say, of your piety? Could you pray in the name of Rev. Moon?

*Lloyd Eby:* Yes, in the name of his position actually, more than in the name of his person.

*Christa Dabeck:* To me it seems that God appoints central people through history, and whether they will be the Messiah or not depends upon whether the establishment of the Kingdom of Heaven happens. Maybe you've heard this over and over again, but it's very real to me. To me, Rev. Moon is the potential Messiah.

*Diana Muxworthy:* What I believe is that he can establish the Kingdom of Heaven on earth. To me, he has been anointed by God to deliver this truth to mankind. He is a union of the word and the deed, and for that reason, he's a Messiah figure. But for me, the test will be whether the Kingdom of Heaven on earth is established or not.

*Dr. Richardson:* Now, I'll just say one thing about this. One of the things that I've learned from this kind of discussion is that the questions we Christian theologians ask are raised out of traditional Christian theology. We're asking, "Whom do you say that he is? Is he the Christ or not?" We're coming from that traditional Christian kind of theology where we say, "I believe Jesus is the Christ, and He has uttered the Word." Now, I don't see that as the way this group works. It seems to me that here's a place where one has to fear biased theology. Let me just pick up what Diana said. The question isn't whether he's the Christ; the question is whether the Kingdom of God is established on earth or not. To the question "Do you believe Rev. Moon is the Messiah?" the answer is not yes or no; the answer is that I feel that I am able now to live better since I understand God's purpose more clearly, etc. The test of whether he's the Messiah or not is not what these people say about Moon, but whether they themselves are living in a transformed way. I think even we see that the impact of these people on us is not directly related to what they believe about Rev. Moon. We keep saying that we're impressed with the kind of people here, and with the kind of life they live. My testimony would be: I don't know whether Moon is the Messiah or not, but I feel a certain strength, invigoration, and clarity about a number of theological ideas. I think you can say it's not just Moon, but something out of this group that has made me a better person. I think that's the form in which the answer to the Messianic question is proposed by this group. That is essentially their offering. If we were to talk about it in the terms of modern theology, we would say they are attempting to get away from understanding faith as a mission of doctrine which is essentially what we're pushing on them. Rather, they are trying to get to faith as life lived in the Kingdom way. I think that's the whole mood of modern theology, and that's what makes this movement very, very modern.

*Dr. Sawatsky:* One problem here. I don't know that that's the direction of the question because I don't think that's a sufficient test: that people just make a confession that they're now living in the Kingdom way. I think you're right that by coming here, we experience something unique or something that's very appealing or affecting or something like that. But I know a lot of people who say that they live in a Kingdom way, and that's not a sufficient answer. I think what we're trying to elicit is some peculiar kind of understanding that cannot be articulated here.

*Dr. Clark:* It doesn't seem to me it's so different from what the early Christians experienced. They lived as if the Kingdom were there in the hope that imminently it was going to be consummated. I guess one will have to know more about what exactly the signs and marks of the coming of the Kingdom are going to be in their external forms, rather than simply talking of transformed life as if the Kingdom has fully dawned.

*Lloyd Eby:* I want to respond to what you were saying. Suppose I believed in establishing the Kingdom and so on, but I just don't accept Rev. Moon. Well, that's really okay. If you're willing, let's build the Kingdom of God. If Rev. Moon is the central figure in that project, then I think it will become apparent at some point. I'm not worried about whether you think it's so now or not. And in fact, if it turns out not to be so, if the Kingdom gets built, that's okay, too. In a sense, it's too bad if you don't believe in Rev. Moon because then you might be able to do more to build the Kingdom than you would if you go on an independent track. I think we're clear that the main thing is accomplishing a new lifestyle. There's no point in making some kind of faith test of whether you're in or out. The point is, what are we going to do together? We'll see what we have when we get there.

*Dr. Sawatsky:* What if I start a new group called the anti-Moon Unification Church?

*Lloyd Eby:* Now that would be counter-productive. (laughter) Don't attack the Unification Church. If you have a better idea about how to build the Kingdom — and Rev. Moon has said this — go ahead. If Rev. Moon finds out yours is better than his, he'll follow you. He has said that over and over, and I think he's sincere. I'd like to emphasize again that it's not any one isolated element that answers this question. For example, living in a Kingdom way is a pretty important part, but it's much more than that. I think when we say we test the Principle, we test it against our reading of the Bible, the Koran, the Bhagavadgita, and every other religion, and against history and what we know of human nature. If we all come to the Principle and accept it because we have come to an understanding already, that shows us that the Principle answers a lot of questions we had and puts together a lot of pieces that were isolated. Then, in combination with the example of Rev. Moon, these things all work together.

72                                    EXPLORING UNIFICATION THEOLOGY

*Jonathan Wells:* I would like to say that I believe that as Unification ideas are accepted, and as individuals try to actualize
them, they will learn from their own experience that Rev. Moon is
the model. He's the one who showed me that it can be done. Now,
the only way anybody can learn whether or not that's true is to try
it in their own life. You don't have to be part of the Church, but if
you try to live the *Divine Principle,* you'll find out that he has done
it and made it possible for you to do it. The *Divine Principle* is not
just intellectual, it's a guide to dynamic, revolutionary action.

*Lokesh Mazumdar:* Let me say something, just briefly. My
parents were Hindus. I grew up in a Hindu home. The school was a
Salesian Catholic school, and I went there for twelve years. I was
not indoctrinated, and I went for one year to a Jesuit college. Most
of the people in my class in school were either Protestant Christians or Catholics or Hindus or Sikhs, or Zoroastrian. Okay, that
is my general background. (laughter) Then I came to America.
When I was introduced to the *Divine Principle* lectures, I just re-
fused to hear. Why? Because I thought they were going to convert
me to Judaism because they were talking about Abraham, Isaac,
Jacob. I was expecting something of a universal nature, and I just
couldn't get beyond that point. I just stopped at Moses. (laughter)
After that, when the talk drifted over to the New Testament and
what that means, I felt that everything was beyond my conception,
my imagination, and my background. Yet something told me that
I had to go beyond my limits. Finally, I was able to see very faint-
ly. I was able to see that this in fact goes beyond Judaism, and goes
beyond Christianity, and goes beyond Hinduism and goes beyond
Sikhism. I was able to see that the Unification Church movement
was struggling to get up from the tribal level to an international
level. Some Christians can understand the whole of the Principle in
one sitting, but a Hindu cannot. He's going to have to accept a lot
of things, hash out a lot of things, and dig into a lot of foreign
ideas. However, I would like to stress that beyond the people involved, beyond the theology involved, there is a certain spiritual
pressure, a spiritual presence that is, I think, the Spirit of God. Because of the Spirit, all people can come to an understanding of the
Principle.

*Jonathan Wells:* I've noticed one thing about Rev. Moon in
his behavior and his teaching. Ask him a theoretical question and
he somehow always gives you a practical answer. With the exception of something like the Madison Square Garden speech which is
a theoretical speech, he is constantly giving practical advice or giving challenges to activity. He never talks about theoretical things

apart from practical things. There's something about his mind that works that way. He has a very practical mind, a mind in which theory and practice are intricately bound together. You can't separate them.

*Lynn Kim:* As Jon was saying, the *Divine Principle* is in a sense, Rev. Moon, and is in a sense autobiographical. We talk about history and the course of Moses and Cain and Abel and Abraham. These figures in the Old Testament and the New Testament are, in a sense, prototypes for the kind of struggle we have to go through ourselves. The struggle between Cain and Abel happens first on an individual level. How can I subjugate what in me is more ungodly and let the godly take over inside myself? Then, in relation to another person, I'm Cain sometimes and sometimes I'm Abel. I have to restore these relationships. And then you move to more and more complex levels. Somehow, symbolically, you relive the whole of the divine principle. When you understand Rev. Moon's personal life and the course that he's gone through, you see that every ounce of his personal testimony *is* the divine principle. He has lived Cain and Abel, he has lived the course of Jacob, he has lived the path of Jesus. So in that sense, the truth of the divine principle is in the living of it.

*Dr. Klaaren:* In a sense, what we've been talking about is what is new. Some people say that what's new is Rev. Moon. Others have other ideas. What is new in this movement? One way to come at that is not to look at ideas, but to look at what you are doing in the light of what I want to call the central ritual of your movement. If you look at classical Catholic Christianity, you see that the sacraments taken during the Mass are the central corporate ritual on which everything rests. There are periods in Catholic theology or in Catholic history when even theology seems a kind of commentary on the Mass. In classical Protestantism like Lutheranism and Calvinism, the central ritual is preaching. Preaching is so central that people in those traditions don't even see it as a ritual, as a symbolic way of talking about God. Then there's another tradition in which the gathering of people themselves in the name of Jesus or of the Spirit is seen to be the primary ritual. This is so for the Anabaptists, so that the worst thing we could do to a person is put a ban on him and put him outside the community. That amounts to putting him out of the church. I'm not looking at things theologically, but rather taking a perspective from the history of religion. From that perspective, what's new about your movement?

*Lynn Kim:* I think one of the simple things would be the stress on the family. You do not enter heaven as an individual, but you enter heaven as a family. Integral to your spiritual development is the entire family experience, particularly the development of the parental heart. We feel that the family is an eternal bond, an eternal relationship that will continue. Now we seem to be a community of individuals, but that's a temporary stage. We see nuclear families developing their relationship, but not closing in on themselves. The family is moving in God's direction. Through the father and the mother particularly, as far as we understand God as being both masculine and feminine, God can manifest His heart fully in the world around Him. Then this God-centeredness will multiply into communities of families.

*Diana Muxworthy:* In one sense, I think that the family emphasis is not really so new as it is a revival. I think that the kind of things that we're trying to do, for example, seeking God on an individual level, are not really new. Men throughout history have sought a deeper relationship with God. We want to see that manifested on many different levels, and so we're working in an active way to first develop our relationship with God and then to multiply that spirit out from families, to the society, nation and world. I don't see it as being necessarily any different than what the Christians wanted to establish. I think the Christians were prevented from expanding on more than the church level. I can't say that we're new, we are just redoing what was the original desire of Christianity.

*Lloyd Eby:* I'm not sure that we really have a central ritual. But there's a sense in which we have marriage as the central ritual. If you want a central ritual, that's it. Yet there's a sense in which each of the things that we do is at least for that time, for that place, a kind of central ritual. We would feel that whatever we're doing at a particular time in a particular place should be a kind of ritual. We do have a very strong sense of commitment to the family.

*Dr. Sawatsky:* Can I make one observation? It would seem to me that that question about the central ritual would have to be answered in relation to the timetable that we're dealing with here. It seems that many ritual elements from other traditions get brought into this, but they get transformed, partly in relation to time. You know, we've always had families. That's not a new idea; but it becomes a very new idea when it is brought into the context of the Third Adam. There are certain possibilities that open up.

*Dr. Klaaren:* That's right. It's similar to the result of classical Protestantism. It isn't that Protestants give up sacraments, nor that they cut the number from seven to two, but that they re-orient what they do sacramentally according to the Word. I would like to ask what's new in ritual and practice here.

*Lynn Kim:* What do you mean by ritual?

*Dr. Klaaren:* Well, I mean rituals like the sacraments or the Mass. A Jesuit priest says the Mass practically every day and his whole life is centered on that. I know a lot of Protestants who not only preach every Sunday, but seem to preach all week long, too. (laughter) There's a primary way of relating to God which stands forth in these different traditions, and I'm not clear what that is for you folks.

*Diana Muxworthy:* I'd like to give my own view. I attend an Episcopal Church every Sunday. The Episcopal ceremony is an hour long, but the minister can only speak fifteen minutes. Rev. Moon sometimes talks four or five hours at a time. So I began to think about liturgy and ritual and our Church. I began to realize that the new ritual which we have is the fact that there is no ritual, that one's own life is the ritual. Right now, to me, ritual is a lot of baloney if there's not a commitment in your inner heart to what is going on at that time. I see Rev. Moon and God and the *Divine Principle* asking me to live what I believe. We have a service with Rev. Moon on Sundays in New York. There is no ritual other than singing and praying and listening to him, and then, immediately after that, going back to work to establish the Kingdom of Heaven on earth. That is the ritual. But I see now, of course, that things like the wedding ceremony can be seen as a ritual. This morning we woke up for Pledge Service at five o'clock, which is, you know, a service which we offer God on Sundays as a sacrifice of our sleep. Witnessing is a ritual too. It's the work that we're doing to establish the Kingdom on earth, and to practice what we speak.

*Joe Stenson:* I just have one thing to say. I think that the rituals in traditional Christianity are the physical acts which connect you with Jesus, through the Catholic Communion and the preaching of the Word. I think the ritual that's most profoundly enacted in each of our individual minds is a living of a life in relationship to Rev. Moon and what he represents which is the coming of the Kingdom. He is the man who is spearheading the way towards the Kingdom of Heaven, and I think our ritual is life in connection with the person who is the central figure.

*Lokesh Mazumdar:* I want to point out one thing that brings out the difficulty of this issue. One should view this in two contexts: one is the context before the Restoration, and one is the context after the Restoration. Quite often we're asked this question: Can you point to something as a sign of the Kingdom? What is the manifestation of the Kingdom? If I could open my heart and if my heart were good enough, that might be a sign. But quite often, we don't have anything to point to. We don't say, "Well, now, here's our community, we're living such and such a way, we're self-sufficient in this aspect, and we have a dynamic relationship with one another." I wouldn't be able to point to somebody and say, "See that person carrying the box of candy, that's the embodiment of the Kingdom." (laughter) It's hard to say "This is what life is going to be like in the Kingdom: you'll be witnessing from six in the morning (laughter), or teaching the *Divine Principle.*" You know, what kind of a kingdom is it where you're giving lectures all day long? (laughter) So, a substantial part of the movement at this time is engaged in the work. This work is somewhat different from living the life in the Kingdom. It's working toward that. Now, it is hoped by God, I'm sure by Rev. Moon, and by most of us that we will be restored. The seeds of the Kingdom are planted inside, and eventually will grow and take root in and around us.

*Joe Stenson:* If there is a ritual to be pointed to, then perhaps we would speak of the wedding ceremony which, as I mentioned yesterday, combines a lot of elements of different sacraments. But our understanding of ritual is, I think, different from the various traditional views. The Catholics view the ritual itself as giving one life. The ritual gives life to you so you go to Mass every Sunday, and if you miss a Sunday, you've lost standing with God. With our view of ritual, I think that the reality of the relationship with God is already established, and the ritual is just a statement of that. We come together and we symbolically go through various actions that state what has already happened. For instance, someone might have already reached a point where he should be married, and say, for various reasons, that can't take place. It might be postponed a year or so. But he has nevertheless already arrived at that point. His relationship with God is already developed to that point. So the ritual itself doesn't give life, but states what has already happened.

But I do agree with the others: our central task is the building of the Kingdom of God.

*Jonathan Wells:* According to the *Divine Principle,* this age is the age when the spiritual and the physical come together. I would say that it is happening now. The very essence of establishing the Kingdom of Heaven on earth is that of putting those two worlds together.

*Klaus Lindner:* The Kingdom of Heaven that we are expecting is actually nothing other than what should have come into existence if the Fall hadn't happened. The Kingdom of Heaven on earth is the perfection of the principle of creation, for example, individual perfection, perfection of the family, perfection of the relationship of man and the universe.

*Dr. Sawatsky:* What are the institutions in the orders of creation? Obviously, the family. Is the state part of the Fall, or is it part of the created order? My assumption is that it's part of the created order in Unification thought.

*Farley Jones:* Our vision is a world without national boundaries. There might be some administrative boundaries, but we have a vision of a world without state boundaries.

*Rev. Calitis:* There are some things I don't understand when you talk about creation. Creation means things like flowers, birds, trees, hills, my wrinkles, my height, my weight, and St. Paul says that these things will not inherit the Kingdom, but that they will all be transformed. St. Paul is quite clear, you know, when he's talking to people who are dying. Before the *parousia,* Paul is saying, "Well, don't worry, nobody has an advantage, because you're all going to be transformed." What's going to happen to the hills, what's going to happen to the trees, and what's their point and what's the point of people who are still living in this world in relation to those who are in the spiritual world?

*Lloyd Eby:* Why don't we turn this question around and ask what your vision of the Kingdom of Heaven is? And why don't you go out and work to build it? This is more important than the question, "What's it going to look like?" I think that it's something that encompasses everything. Creation clearly is not just the flowers and trees and grass, but also the buildings because every created activity is a part of God's creation working through man.

*Rev. Calitis:* That's fair enough, Lloyd, what I'm getting at is a certain confusion — at least ambiguity — that runs through your talk about the Kingdom of Heaven on earth. You seem to take the language of eschatology very literally. Rather than understanding Paul's language as meaning, symbolically, that there will come a future state when God's relationship to His creation will be dramatically altered. You take that language literally. Aren't you confusing two modes of discourse: the literal and the symbolic?

*Klaus Lindner:* There are actually two Kingdoms of Heaven. There is a Kingdom of Heaven on earth, and one after we die. Once the Kingdom of Heaven on earth is established, there will still be a Kingdom of Heaven after we die. If those two are not distinguished, a confusion arises.

*Joe Stein:* We combine both kinds of discourse. The reason is our view of the messianic mission is both spiritual and physical. When we discuss the mission of Jesus, we say that He came not only to create a spiritual Kingdom, but to create a physical Kingdom. The concept of transformation for us would basically move in the direction of the right use of individuals and creation. It is not a view of bodies and trees suddenly changed into spiritual matter. The world as it is has the capacity to be the Kingdom of Heaven on earth if we rightly use it.

*Dr. Bryant:* Is your view of the Kingdom on earth centered on the change of attitudes or the change of structures? The way you are talking now sounds like you are a group that puts the change of attitudes first. Once you get right relationships with God on the level of the individual and families, then the Kingdom has come. The world then remains essentially unchanged structurally. It's just that it's occupied by good people, God-centered people. Is that your view? Would you have businesses that are like other businesses and schools that are like other schools, with the difference being that no one will be cheating and no one will be dishonest? If that is your view, it does not seem to recognize the stubbornness of the world of social institutions. It seems naive. For example, do you really believe that working in Budd Automotive in Kitchener, Ontario, is building the Kingdom of God and that the only problem with Budd Automotive is that the people working there don't have the right kind of spiritual relationship with God? And if they had that, they would be happy to work at Budd Automotive because that's the way we're producing cars for people to drive around in? Is that your view?

*Linda Mitchell:* May I respond to that? I've thought about that. I don't think that any of us has a final answer. I think that this is pure speculation on our part. The one thing that I see happening within our movement at this time is that one person does not always dig ditches, and another person always does another thing. But our view is centered in a sharing of the joy and burdens of building a society together. Once we're in the middle of the Kingdom of Heaven a certain number of people would still have to do automotive work. If you have to be there, if you have to spend one month in an automotive factory, I don't think it would destroy you. I think that all people can experience joy even in doing those not-so-pleasurable things. We can experience joy because we're doing it for the sake of other people, and doing it with a different heart.

*Dr. Bryant:* So the structures, the institutions are okay?

*Linda Mitchell:* No. But the heart of the problem is our relationships with God and others.

*Dr. Bryant:* In the Kindom of God on earth, do people continue to die?

*Lloyd Eby:* Yes, sure.

*Dr. Sawatsky:* But people will not be sorrowful over death? There will be no tears?

*Linda Mitchell:* Right. The spiritual world is much greater and much broader and more beautiful than the physical world.

*Dr. Sawatsky:* Do those in the spiritual world live through the goings on of the physical world?

*Linda Mitchell:* Not necessarily. This earth is the scene of the process of restoration. Man's purpose on earth is to grow to perfection, then to have a family, and then to fulfill his responsibilities for the world. Once man has done that, then he can go on to the spiritual world and live a much fuller, more beautiful life.

*Dr. Clark:* What happens to people who die before they fulfill any or all of the blessings?

*Mike Jenkins:* They work through people who are here, cooperating with and helping them. By helping them, by trying to influence them in some way, they can also receive the benefits of their earthly partner. Also, I've begun to realize that if what I believe is that the spirit is eternal, then eternal life is even more real than my own lifetime.

*Dr. Bryant:* Okay, I can get that, but one of the things that now starts to slip away is the notion of a physical restoration that I thought was so absolutely central to Unification thought. Instead, it sounds like the world remains as it is, but our attitudes change. The first time we talked about physical restoration it sounded like you expected some actual transformation of human nature and the world. As Juris once asked, "Do perfected people get colds?" Certainly, when you talk about a physical restoration and perfection it sounds like it should entail a change in our fleshly nature; and now it sounds like it's getting very spiritualized again, that it's simply a God-centered relation. Am I misunderstanding you?

*Tirza Shilgi:* I think that you confuse two things. I think that there's a physical world and a spiritual world, both of which existed from the beginning. Restoration has to be accomplished in both the physical world and the spiritual world. Because of the Fall, fallen people have gone to the spirit world. Therefore, all the consequences of the Fall are there as well. Both the physical and spiritual worlds are in need of restoration. We don't know about the spiritual world in any detail. But we do know that the main essence of the restoration is the correction of the order of things, the internal order of things. The Fall introduced a certain self-centeredness which started to draw energy and love inwardly, into people. People became preoccupied with consuming things. People therefore became deprived of things: deprived of love, deprived of this and that, because everyone acted like a drain. The whole theme of restoration is a reversal of this pattern so that a person will be a source of love and energy rather than a drain of love and energy. With this internal reordering, things would start moving in a much more harmonious way, the way they do, for example, in nature. In nature, things correspond to that principle of give-and-take. I believe that this is the very purpose of being. When that order will be changed we don't know in detail. It will take time and we will have difficulties. We will experience hardships, but there will be a point behind it; things will be moving towards their right order.

*Lloyd Eby:* Besides, you have to understand that things are not singular, but dual. Duality runs through everything, so that if you think in only spiritual terms or in only physical terms, you make a mistake. You must understand that when we're talking about spiritual things, in the Unification view, we're simultaneously talking about physical things because they belong together.

*Jonathan Wells:* I agree. And I'd like to add that spiritual effort is directly and immediately manifested on a physical level. For example, you can go down to 42nd Street in New York City and look at a junkie standing on the sidewalk. Look in his face. What you see is a reflection of his spirituality. Then look at one of us. We're not perfect, but we're a lot different from that junkie, and it's visible. There is a difference, and it's visibly manifested; and the Kingdom of Heaven is manifested in this way, too.

*Rev. Calitis:* But let's be clear where my question comes from. The Christian vision it seems to me is that at one point, the thing that is mortal, the created order, will achieve immortality; and that will be done by a transformation which will create a new heaven and new earth which is one single thing, rather than two types of things.

*Lloyd Eby:* But in Unification, it is one single thing. But any single thing contains two aspects.

*Rev. Calitis:* Yes, but in your view everything is to be done by the sweat of your brow and is possible. But aren't material things really in opposition to spiritual purposes? I know that my body doesn't express all that I'd like it to express spiritually. I blush. I can't run as fast as I'd like. My body is supposed to be for relating to others and in fact, it distances me from others, because it isn't a perfect expression of the spirit. Where do we find a body which is a perfect expression of the spirit? In the Christian tradition, the view has been that this perfect harmony of body and spirit is not achievable through the cells and the chemistry of our bodies as presently constituted. Rather the belief is that we would have to have a rather colossal transformation: not just one that can be worked out in history, but one that is achieved by an act of God, a creative act of God again.

*Lloyd Eby:* Right, and I think that same thing exists here. In Unification theology the restoration can't be accomplished apart from the person of the Lord of the Second Advent.

*Farley Jones:* I'd like to say something. I don't think we envision the Kingdom of God to be the world as it is with individuals having different attitudes. We believe that at the point when people come into a fuller relationship with God, with their own true and original natures, they will create a very different kind of world on earth, very different from what we have now. We'll create a world that reflects the original beauty and purity of the human spirit. Thus, for example, New York City will not be New York City as we know it. Cities, if we even have cities, will be very different places.

*Dr. Bryant:* That's very important. I would hope that the Unification notion of the Kingdom of God on earth would not include a lot of things like Budd Automative. (laughter) At the same time, this gives us some insight into why you people are so anti-Communist. You see them as rivals. As Professor Richardson mentioned earlier, the Christian churches don't have a socio-political alternative. The force in the modern world that you see as a rival is Communism. They have a secular Kingdom of God on earth that's coming, and they've got a way to get to it. Most Christians, on the other hand, don't hold that notion anymore. Their Kingdom of God is beyond this world.

*Tom Selover:* That's why the final teaching about how to overcome Communism is not through war. We want to do what they want to do, but on the right foundation. Most people become Communists, it seems to me, because of a desire for social transformation. And we're aiming at that too, but on a God-centered foundation.

# THE DIVINE PRINCIPLE:
# TEXT AND PRINCIPLE

*Dr. Bryant:* Let's get straight about the status and transmission of the text of the *Divine Principle.*

*Lloyd Eby:* There's an interesting sentence that occurs in the Black Book. It's the last paragraph on page 16. It says that the divine principle revealed in this book is only part of the new truth. "We have recorded here what Sun Myung Moon's disciples have hitherto heard and witnessed, and we believe the happy expectation that as time goes on, deeper parts of the truth will be continually revealed . . ." I take it to mean that one can distinguish between the divine principle as a principle and the expression of the divine principle which is in the book.

*Klaus Lindner:* Rev. Moon says that we cannot really *know* God, although we can experience God. The *Divine Principle* can only give us symbols and images. These can only point to the divine principle underlying the book.

*Dr. Bryant:* Could one say, then, what the divine principle is? It seems that it's there in the book, but it's not there.

*Lloyd Eby:* I think the divine principle is that principle by which God exists, by which God creates, by which God restores mankind. The divine principle is not synonymous with God. But one could say that it's God's *logos.* Anything that one discovers which is true is, in my opinion, an aspect of the divine principle. For example, all of the scientific truths which will be discovered in the future are parts of the divine principle because they're expressions of God's creativity.

*Dr. Wilson:* But all this can change because what's considered truth by the last generation's assumptions may not be considered truth by this generation's assumptions.

*Lloyd Eby:* Yes, that's a problem.

*Dr. Wilson:* I know a physiologist who was the head of the Physiology Department at Mayo. He says that he has been in physiology over forty years, and half of what he learned he now knows is false.

*Lloyd Eby:* Yes, there's that problem. My own way of solving that problem would be to start talking about scientific theories as an approximation of truth that one gets through the development of science. Insofar as there are any scientific truths, and I take it that there are some, the process of scientific discovery is a process of coming to something which is a nearer and nearer approximation of the truth. Those things are parts of the divine principle. I give science just as an example to show how encompassing, at least for me, the notion of a divine principle is.

*Dr. Wilson:* How do you distinguish this from pantheism?

*Lloyd Eby:* Well, presumably pantheism would be the claim that everything is God. I haven't said that everything is God. I'd say that all truths are part of God's *logos,* which is quite a different thing.

*Dr. Bryant:* Let's try to stay on the divine principle. Let's try some other sacred literature. We do for example have the statements in the *Divine Principle* that the *Divine Principle* is the completion of the Old and New Testaments. As a completion, I would imagine it has a higher status for members of the Unification Church than, say, the Old or New Testament.

*Linda Mitchell:* It seems to me that the *Divine Principle* is very different from the Bible. It seems to me that people take the Bible word by word and each word is interpreted in and of itself. The *Divine Principle* is, and people can correct me if I'm wrong, the completion of the Old and New Testaments in a special sense. It is a clearer explanation of what we feel God is revealing in the Old and New Testaments. So it wouldn't contradict the Old and New Testaments. We feel it is a clarification of the Old and New Testaments. It's my opinion that the *Divine Principle* is written down in this form as a way to spread the word and to teach the divine principle. But the *Divine Principle* doesn't appear to me to be completed. It is not a finished work of theological affirmation.

*Dr. Vander Goot:* There is this analogy, though, with the Christian Scriptures. The Bible is often called the Word of God, but the Bible is only the Word of God in a secondary sense, because the Word of God is in the creation, and in the person of Jesus Christ. The Bible is the Word of God in the same sense that this book is the divine principle. It is the lingual, symbolical representation of that which is beyond it, yet in which it is grounded. And I sense, too, that you believe that the *Divine Principle* is not just the *logos* of God but also the *eros:* that is, it is clearly more than the structure of the universe; it's also the dynamic movement of the universe from beginning to end. It seems that it is the *logos* and *eros* of the entire cosmos.

*Linda Mitchell:* We believe that the divine principle is the principle by which God creates and the principle by which man should live. If these two are united, then joy and beauty can happen. But when man is living by a principle which deviates from God's principle of creation, then you have what you have today.

*Dr. Bryant:* Earlier, Linda, you spoke about rewriting the *Divine Principle.* Can you expand on that?

*Linda Mitchell:* This is only my speculation. I've had the feeling that although the Black Book edition is the essence of the *Divine Principle,* I wouldn't feel uncomfortable if there was a sentence that was changed. I believe that the *Divine Principle,* as well as Miss Kim's book that came before that, is adequate to explain the divine principle. So we have the essence of the divine principle, but I would hesitate to claim that it can never change. I don't think that it necessarily has to or that it's not true, but I think that there is still a possibility of more being added.

*Dr. Sawatsky:* Is the distance of the Black Book version of the *Divine Principle* from the original text seen as a problem? Is there a sense of an original text?

*Lynn Kim:* At this point, no to both questions.

*Diana Muxworthy:* We don't have to study Korean to understand the *Divine Principle.*

*Lynn Kim:* I think that if one understood Korean, one could understand the *Divine Principle* with more depth. Since it is not symbolic like the Bible, since it's more systematic and straightforward, the problem of translation is a minor one.

For one thing, Rev. Moon is still with us, so if we have a question we can ask him. The problem of an authoritative text isn't widely felt, at least not yet.

*Dr. Sawatsky:* Is this because you still have a living tradition?

*Lynn Kim:* Yes, I think so.

*Farley Jones:* During the weekend, I've gotten the impression that we were leading some of our guests to think that the principle as a theological system is still in a process of formulation and evolution, that the concepts, in the *Divine Principle,* will be changed. If anybody has gotten that impression, I think it's inaccurate. I can see that some of the wording may be modified, but I don't think we should assume it's going to happen. I do think that what's in the Black Book is basically what we have to deal with. We don't necessarily see a time when we will sit down as theologians and rewrite the *Divine Principle*. There may come a time when individuals will develop different theological concepts within the Principle, but that the actual book itself will be reworked or rewritten conceptually is not our expectation.

*Mike Jenkins:* I fully expect it to be rewritten. (laughter) When I look at that book I know in my heart that that's not the final written document expressing the divine principle in English. I don't believe that that will become the canonized text. Rev. Moon himself has said that some day he would like to write it himself. On the other hand, I think Lloyd is saying that God or God's divine principle of action and work, His existence, His essence, is something that is within God and does not change. The way God functions in the world is something that is unchanging. But the *Divine Principle* uses analogies, pictures and examples that are common to everyone's life, and these certainly can be presented in different forms with different examples. The essence, I think, remains the same as is contained in the principle of creation, fall, and restoration.

*Jonathan Wells:* It seems to me that if Rev. Moon were to rewrite the *Divine Principle* his rewriting of it might, in fact, be more controversial than this version. I think we should understand that.

*Rev. Calitas:* In what sense do you anticipate a more controversial version?

*Jonathan Wells:* I don't mean that it will be. What I am saying is that if the rewriting were to take place under Rev. Moon's direction, it wouldn't be to calm the popular controversy that the book has aroused. That's what I mean.

*Dr. Bryant:* One thing that's striking to me about the *Divine Principle* is its form. As a sacred text (at least for this community) I can't think of any other sacred texts that are quite like this one. The more common form is stories.

This is the only *sacred* text that I know that simultaneously discloses a revelation and attempts to formulate the revelation in categories that then are inexplicably linked with that revelation. Isn't that rather peculiar? Are there other texts like this one?

*Lokesh Mazumdar:* I would say that we don't really look upon the Book as a *sacred* Book. It's not a sacred text. The point was made, sometime last year, that many theologians wouldn't read the *Divine Principle* because it was written in seventeenth century language. I can see something to that. I don't know if that's true or not, but if it is, I could easily imagine a group of people coming together and saying, "Let's rewrite the principle in twentieth century language." Now, I don't think that doing that necessarily means changing the divine principle or anything of that kind. The principle will still be the principle, regardless of whether we understand it, or whether we put it down correctly, or whether anybody changes it. That's the way I feel. But it just may be true that it is seventeenth century language, and that people can't relate to that kind of stuff. So I would say develop it, yes, add on to it, yes, but as far as changing the basic structure of the principle, no, that's impossible.

*Dr. Bryant:* Lokesh, you're saying that the divine principle is the divine principle is the divine principle. Are you saying that the divine principle is in that book, but it's not in the words in that book?

*Lokesh Mazumdar:* It's not restricted to the words.

*Dr. Vander Goot:* Let me try. The problem is with the word "principle." Principle, in this context, is not an idea or notion that we have in our minds that we now have to live by or put into practice. In this context, a principle is something that possesses us; it's not something that we possess. This book merely points to that which is beyond it, namely, the organizational dynamic and structure of the cosmos. There is an unfortunate ambiguity in the word principle. Generally we tend to understand "principle" to mean some kind of notion that we have to put into practice. That is clearly not what it means here.

*Klaus Lindner:* Can I say something? At the time when I joined the Unification movement in Germany, we did not have the Black Book edition of the *Divine Principle.* Then we had a smaller, red version of the *Divine Principle* by Dr. Kim. And we had the *Study Guide* that's written by President Kim, the present President of the Unification Church. I must say that I had no sense that any of those three, quite different, expressions of the divine principle was more authoritative. When we studied the *Study Guide,* we felt that it expressed the divine principle more clearly. But none of them contradict each other on doctrinal points.

*Dr. Vander Goot:* It's interesting that there's no doctrine about the Book within the Book itself. (laughter) It has all kinds of doctrines, but that one is absent.

*Dr. Richardson:* The fact of the matter is that there are different versions with different emphases in different versions. Eventually you're going to have to face this problem. That is, a critical, analytical, theological intelligence is going to examine the organi-

zation of each version to see what's in and what's left out. It's like
Calvin and predestination. Is predestination the heart of Calvinism
or isn't it? Well, somebody says, look at where it is in the first edition and look where it comes in the last edition. Calvin organized
them in different ways and it becomes a doctrine for reassurance
rather than a metaphysical doctrine. You're going to have to face
these problems. What you're going to end up with, of course, is
fifteen or twenty different authoritative versions of the *Divine
Principle,* in each of which the principle is fully and completely
contained, although they all contradict one another. (laughter)

*Tom Selover:* I don't think Unificationism is ever going to be
a book religion.

*Lloyd Eby:* I'd like to say something about the relationship of
this book to the Old Testament and New Testament. Jesus was
faced with the problem of the Old Testament Scriptures, and He
said that the real key to understanding those scriptures is understanding me; I'm the one who tells you what those things were really trying to say. I think the same thing is true here. This is the thing
that tells you what the Old and New Testament are really trying to
say, so if you see an inconsistency, the problem isn't the inconsistency, the problem is your understanding of the Old and New
Testament.

*Dr. Bryant:* If there's anything in the Scriptures, in the Old
and New Testament, which contradicts the *Divine Principle,* now
we know where the error is. The error, in your view, is in the Old
and New Testament; it's not in the *Divine Principle.*

*Jonathan Wells:* Don't we have to take the Old and New Testament and understand why a particular passage was written? For
example, in Romans, Paul says that we should live by faith. And in
James we read that faith without works is dead. Well, you can understand these two passages to be contradictory if you want to.
There are many other examples in the Bible. But if Paul was talking to somebody who overemphasized the law, then of course that
person had to be raised in his faithfulness. If James was talking to
someone who threw everything into the faith and neglected worldly duties altogether, then that person had to be corrected. And we
understand Jesus' words in the same respect. When He talked to
the rich young man and told him to give away his wealth, He
wasn't saying that in every case the route to God was to give your
money to the poor, but *your* route to God is to get rid of your
hangup by giving your money to the poor and following Him. My
point is that we have to understand the context.

And Jesus had to say there are no other Messiahs but Me, because there were lots of other messiahs, and they were all false messiahs in those days. But it's also possible to read passages in the New Testament that predict a future Messiah who is not Jesus Himself.

*Dr. Bryant:* In the Bible?

*Jonathan Wells:* Sure, in Revelations.

*Dr. Bryant:* In Revelations, it says "Come, Lord Jesus."

*Jonathan Wells:* Well, this is where we get into the interpretation. I interpret it differently. I did even before I read the *Divine Principle.*

*Lloyd Eby:* I want to say something else about this relationship. I'll try to be a little more subtle than I was before. That is, I understand that Rev. Moon has said that you should be able to understand the *Divine Principle,* or at least significant parts of it, by really understanding the Old and New Testaments. In other words, I don't really believe in emphasizing the discontinuity; I want to emphasize the continuity between them. I want to say that this principle, this divine principle, not the book, but this divine *logos* and *eros,* has been operating throughout all of history, throughout the whole creation. There is an expression of that in the Old and the New Testaments: if one's eyes were open, one would see it.

*Dr. Richardson:* What is this principle that we're supposed to be seeing that's so obvious?

*Lloyd Eby:* I didn't say it's so obvious.

*Dr. Richardson:* Well, I mean, what is it?

*Lloyd Eby:* Well, for example, the whole restoration scheme.

*Dr. Richardson:* Well, Dr. Kim will say that that's not the divine principle. The divine principle is just the principle of creation, and all this historical stuff is speculation.

*Lloyd Eby:* Yes, I know she says that, but I'm not sure I agree with her. I think the principle of restoration is part of the divine principle also.

*Dr. Richardson:* Yes, but don't you see how incredible this is? Here's Dr. Young Kim saying that the Divine Principle is just the principle of creation, and all the rest of that stuff is written by other people and added to it. It's not the revelation of Rev. Moon. Then somebody comes along and says what you're saying, namely, that the divine principle is the principle of restoration. And Dr. Kim says that's not right, it's only the principle of creation. And he says, well, I read the book and I see it's the Principle of Restoration. Not only that, but Lloyd Eby agrees with me. (much laughter)

*Lloyd Eby:* I think that's wrong. I think the principle of creation is the primary thing, and the principle of restoration is something which comes into play after the Fall, so that the principle of restoration is a sub-segment of the divine principle. Primarily the divine principle is the principle of creation.

*Lokesh Mazumdar:* God is using the principle of restoration to bring about salvation, so that becomes the principle of God's salvific work.

*Dr. Richardson:* Yes, but I mean, how many divine principles are there?

# PART II
## FOUR CRITICAL RESPONSES

THE HUMANITY OF GOD AND THE DIVINITY OF MAN:
REFLECTIONS ON UNIFICATION'S
THEOLOGY OF CREATION

Dr. Henry Vander Goot

WOMEN IN THE THEOLOGY
OF THE UNIFICATION CHURCH

Dr. Elizabeth Clark

THE UNIFICATION CHURCH: SOME PRELIMINARY
SUGGESTIONS FOR HISTORICAL AND SOCIAL
SCIENTIFIC ANALYSIS

Dr. Rodney Sawatsky

CRITICAL REFLECTIONS ON
UNIFICATION ESCHATOLOGY

Dr. M. Darrol Bryant

# THE HUMANITY OF GOD AND THE DIVINITY OF MAN: REFLECTIONS ON UNIFICATION'S THEOLOGY OF CREATION

*Henry Vander Goot*

Before I begin to deal with the subject matter proper of this paper, I would like to offer a few general observations about Unification's Theology of Creation as a whole. The first is that Unification theology understands that an adequately theistic system "begins" its theological reflection with the story of Adam and Eve, not with the story of Jesus. Unification thought tries to be a genuinely *theo*logical system, and it realizes that such an intention can only be fulfilled where the various theological *"loci"* are developed from the prospective glance of the doctrine of creation. Any other perspective is necessarily "retrospective," and by that token invariably anthropocentric.

Furthermore, Unification theology also discerns that to lend concreteness to the doctrine of sin and subsequently to the doctrine of salvation, creation must be defined in terms of specific structures. This is where all theological reflection either gets started on an adequate footing or goes amiss. Not only does Unification theology affirm the priority of creation, but it also displays considerable sensitivity to the fact that even the foundational assumption of creation is subject to ideological distortion. If vaguely formulated, the theological assumption of creation is as susceptible of being

All bracketed references are to the *Divine Principle,* 2nd edition, New York: Holy Spirit Association for the Unification of World Christianity, 1973.

swallowed up by an alien structure as Christology and eschatology have been in the contemporary theological discussion. To prevent this, Unification theology sees that the theology of creation must be lent a certain concreteness. An analysis of cosmic structures is required, and Unification's notion of the three four-position bases (of the individual, the family and society) performs this indispensable function. It is at this level that a specific sense is prepared for Unification's subsequent conception of sin and restoration.

Finally, to a considerable extent Unification theology, though it recognizes the indispensability of an analysis of concrete structures, nonetheless has succeeded in preventing its theology from being swallowed up by an alien philosophy. This is indeed unique in the contemporary theological context. The worthiness of contemporary theologies is increasingly judged by the measure to which they can make their concepts concrete without being assimilated to alien philosophical analyses. These philosophical analyses prove to be covers for a narrative portrayal of life which comes into conflict with the theologies to which those philosophical analyses have been attached. In the Protestant and Catholic worlds the search is on for distinctively "Christian" ontologies. Unification theology participates in that search.

Recognizing the crucial relevance of the theology of creation, I should now like to turn to the topic proper of this paper. This topic is the relationship of Unification doctrines of creation and restoration. A rather cursory perusal of the *Divine Principle* makes manifestly obvious the fundamentality of the so-called "Restoration motif" in Unification thought. According to the *Divine Principle,* redemption is the restoration of the original creation; it is emphatically not a radically or absolutely new start.

However much this restoration motif might be attractive — especially to Reformed Calvinists — our enthusiasm must be tempered by a more thorough-going analysis of what specifically is meant by "restoration." Theologically, many options are possible within even a restorationist framework. In other words, we might say that the logical fundamentality of creation in relation to redemption can itself be variously understood.

For example, such widely historically separated and signally different theologians as Irenaeus and Luther formally concur in asserting the theological priority of creation over redemption. Both Irenaeus and Luther share (at least formally speaking) the conviction that salvation can be understood only against the background of God's more primitive work in creation. Yet the specific meaning of this principle of the logical originality of God's work in creation has a different actual meaning in each case. In fact this is already indicated by the use of two distinct terms in their common stress on the essentiality of God's original work: namely "creation" in the case of Irenaeus and "law" in the case of Luther.

Though Irenaeus and Luther stand together over against theologians who "begin" their theological reflection with the story of Jesus, Irenaeus and Luther stand together only in an abstract and formal sense. The specific difference between Irenaeus' conception, on the one hand, and Luther's on the other, must not be neglected.

For Irenaeus the essence of Christianity is best described in terms of the "duality of creation and recapitulation." However, for Luther this same essence is understood in terms of the "dialectic of law and gospel."

In the theology of Irenaeus, recapitulation releases and sets free the uncorrupted life of the original creation. The new is the old, for the goal of salvation is the restoration and re-establishment of the lost goal of creation. For Irenaeus, then, the form of the relationship that exists between creation and redemption is one of harmony, unity and continuity. Recapitulation frees humankind *for creation.*

By contrast, in the case of Luther the essential form of the relation that exists between creation and redemption is conflict. The law-gospel formula stresses the contrast between its two constituent terms. Thus, Luther's formula emphasizes the radical uniqueness of the gospel.

This is not to deny that for Luther law and gospel are in some sense harmonious. They are, indeed, both activities of the same God. They are two ways in which the one God rules. Yet, this dimension of the law-gospel relationship is not the point that qualifies it and lends it its specific sense. The uniqueness of the law-gospel relationship is that the two terms form an antithesis. The law-gospel relationship highlights the principle of dissimilarity. The Word bestows forgiveness, and the law-gospel formula thus stresses man's freedom from the burden of guilt more than his actual possession of new life. The new is opposed to the old, for the old is what is overcome. The gospel frees humankind *from that law.*

My point thus far has been to demonstrate the importance of asking what Unification thought means by "creation" in asserting that salvation is its "restoration." Though it is theologically difficult to quarrel with restorationism as such, the discussion cannot be allowed to end at this point. For the concrete concept of creation involved in Unification thought may itself pose new problems.

For example, my assessment is that Unification theology's concrete concept of creation comes finally to vitiate the restoration motif itself. Unification theology maintains a notion of creation as the differentiation of the inner life of God, a notion that finds no easy reconciliation with the motif of restoration in its most precise sense. Restoration thus becomes "Return to God" in a literal sense, and this is divinization, not the repetition or re-establishment of "creaturehood." In Unification theology restoration cannot be the republication of creaturehood because "creaturehood" is not adequately ontically distinguished from the being of God and cannot be assigned, therefore, an intermediate character or nature of its own. Therefore, the question of how "it" can be "restored" is immediately suggested. The following pages will be devoted to a clarification of this argument.

The *Divine Principle* opens its theological discussion of Unification thought with the idea of the "Dual Characteristics of God." [20] This duality of God is the polarity of positivity and negativity. Furthermore, it is a reciprocal relationship corresponding to the dualities of interiority and exteriority, subject and object, character and form, and masculinity and femininity. [24]

In addition, the *Divine Principle* asserts that the world was created in God's image. Like God, the world displays the polarity of positivity and negativity at the fundamental ontic level. "The Universe," says the *Divine Principle,* ". . . has its own internal character and external form."

But, according to Unification thought, the world is more than a metaphor. It is more than a reflection of the divine life. Indeed, the strong claim is made that the universe has God as its center. The created order is the external form of God; or God is the inner character or deepest energy of the world. Says the *Divine Principle:* "In relation to the whole creation, God is the masculine subject representing its internal character." [25]

Though God is transcendent, according to the *Divine Principle* He is also the *dynamis* of the created order. In fact the *Divine Principle* calls Him the "Universal Prime Energy."

Energy is, of course, motion, not just extension in space and duration in time. In Unification theology the notion of energy (which is God) explains how the creation, though fundamentally and at the highest level of generality intelligible in terms of positivity and negativity, specifically becomes a multiplicity of concrete, dual structures. God's being is the base of the cosmic process through whose "give-and-take" secondary, tertiary and quaternary purposes emerge. Says the *Divine Principle:* "When, through

Universal Prime Energy, the dual essentialities of God enter into give-and-take action by forming a reciprocal relationship, the force of give-and-take action causes multiplication." [31]

Finally, this process of differentiation is designated the "origin-division-union (O-D-U) action." Little has to be said about how basic this three-tiered "ontology" is to Unification thought. It is the overall structural framework within which Unification thought concretely articulates (1) its doctrine of sin as the vitiation of personal integrity, familial order, and social community; (2) its notion of the mission and failure of Israel; (3) its doctrine of the work and failure of Christ; and finally (4) its very this-worldly conception of the personal, familial, and world-political calling of the community of the regenerate. Upon the children of God rests the awesome responsibility of bringing about fulfillment at every level in the wake of the failures that have characterized the past.

Crucial to my purposes is the initial assumption that the three four-position (O-D-U) bases constitute the horizontal structure of creation, and that they are in effect actually (ontologically) the unfolded objectification of the inner life of God Himself. Creation is actually the life of God; or, the inner, dynamic, organizational structure of the universe is the Divine Being Himself.

This theological position is nowhere more vividly indicated than in Unification's conception of God's Joy and Love, and Unification's corresponding notion of the centrality of the base position of family and marriage. The group constituted by God, male and female, and children is the concrete foundation from which the base of human society flows and in terms of which the base of the human constitution (God, mind and body, perfect man) acquires its real significance.

According to Unification thought God is Heart (Love) and His desire is the experience of Joy. God can only fulfill Himself by objectifying Himself in His creation, whose center base is marriage and the family. Only through man, through his experience of love and joy, can God's own desire for fulfillment and Joy be realized. Man is the vehicle through which God (the Lover) relates Himself to the world (the Beloved.)[1]

If man fails, God does not experience Joy. But as man achieves perfection, says Prof. Kim, "the *incarnation* of God is at last fulfilled."[2] As we follow man's efforts to attain to the purpose

---

[1] See Young Oon Kim, *Unification Theology and Christian Thought.* rev. ed. New York: Golden Gate, 1976, pp. 23-25.

[2] *Ibid.,* p. 38, emphasis added.

of creation at every level or base position, we are in effect observing the development of God's own life. The evolution of creation is God's own history.

But this growth of creation is also man's history, man's autobiography. However, since the life of the world is preceded by God and since it comes again to be drawn into Him, man's perfection really comes to life beyond the *restoration* of creaturehood. Says the *Divine Principle:* "The man whose mind and body have formed a four-position foundation of the original God-centered nature becomes God's temple ... and forms one body with Him ... This means that man attains *deity.*" [43, emphasis added.]

Another way of indicating the same thing might be to say that since the life of God is also the life of man, man "precedes" himself and in principle should be destined to become more than he was actually created to be. What he was created to be has no specifiable boundaries. For example, in Unification theology marital love is sacred, so that, as Prof. Kim herself observes, "When a man and woman unite in perfection, they are in a sense *a new higher being* even closer to God."[3]

It should be apparent that Unification theology regards as a single continuous reality the life of God and the being of the creation. If deification is not the final goal of creation, then surely creation is in principle at best only an intermediate and subordinate metaphysical part of the Divine Being.

But what has become here of the notion of Creation? What has become of the idea that God is Creator, not creation? What has become of the idea that there is an absolute void between God and what He calls into being? What has become of the idea that there is nothing in God Himself that can or must ensue in creation? And, if we allow these ideas to disappear, can we still speak in a theologically respectable way of "Creation?"

Furthermore, when the infinite difference between God and His creation is ignored, is not the precise sense of "restoration" also jeopardized? Is it not the case that if God and creation are somehow only interrelated and structured through one another, then the creation can have no finally definable nature, just as God can finally have no incomprehensibility, or dignity and majesty?

It is my impression that if the indelible line of demarcation that separates God from His creation is eclipsed, then restoration cannot be the recapitulation of creaturehood either; for there is

---

[3] *Ibid.,* p. 49.

then no such reality as "creaturehood," at least as distinct from the being of God Himself. Restoration must become the transformation and translation of humanity into the divinity of God. The concrete sense of restoration becomes qualified by the notion of divinization, and restoration becomes specifically "Return to God" in a substantive or metaphysical sense. The notion of "Union with God" is inevitably turned into a cosmological process.

My criticism of Unification theology is that while it tries to honor the language of restoration, it vitiates this effort by failing adequately to honor the ontic difference between God and His creation. This difference is the key assumption of the doctrine of creation. Creation stands or falls with this idea.

Furthermore, the restoration motif goes hand in hand with creation. Where creation becomes confused with the actually incomprehensible majesty of God, creation loses its nature as a "self-identical" reality, and the sense of restoration becomes deification or actual metaphysical "Return to God." Unification theology must choose between creation and restoration on the one hand and the principle of the bi-polarity of the Divine Being in terms of positivity and negativity on the other. The two are incompatible concepts.

## DISCUSSION I

*Lloyd Eby:* I want to ask a question. At the end of your paper you say that "the difference between God and His creation is the key assumption of the doctrine of creation." What is that key?

*Dr. Vander Goot:* I'm talking about classical Christian theology. It seems to me that within Christian thought that assumption has to be made and is the point of the doctrine of creation. God is one thing and that which He calls into being is quite another thing. From the point of view of being, God and Creation do not overlap. God *is* absolutely. There is nothing within Him, or before Him, or alongside Him out of which creation flows. God *is* absolutely. That means in effect, that God is one thing and creation is another.

*Dr. Clark:* Your criticism of Unification thought is that the distinction between the Creator and the creation is confused. Yet when you were speaking I found myself thinking that much of what you said Unification theology is sounds like Greek Orthodox thought. Would you make this same criticism of Greek Orthodox theology?

*Linda Mitchell:* In my understanding, the *Divine Principle* and Greek Orthodox thought seem very close. I understand Greek Orthodoxy to say that there are two aspects of God: His essence and His energies. Man can never become one with God in essence, but he can become one with God's energies. The *Divine Principle* never asserts that man will become one in being with God, but simply that he will be united in heart with God.

*Dr. Vander Goot:* Okay, but how does that stand theologically with the fact that there is the persistent argument in the *Divine Principle* that God is the "Center" of the universe? This is not, it seems to me, a metaphor, but an ontology.

*Dr. Richardson:* How do you differentiate that from the Orthodox way of saying that the world is dependent on God, that man is made in the image of God, that God's purposes are worked out in creation, and so on? Why are you criticizing Unification theology for a way of talking about these considerations that is very much a part of traditional Christian language?

*Dr. Vander Goot:* To say that the creation is totally dependent on God is not to say that there is no distinction between the Creator and creation. It is simply to say that the creation has no absolute identity or being in and of itself, and that creation must constantly be referred to that which lies beyond it.

*Dr. Richardson:* But is it as clear as you assume that the *Divine Principle* confuses creation with Creator? For example, creation falls. There is at least one case in which there obviously is some distinction between God the Creator and His creation.

*Dr. Vander Goot:* Yes, that's true. There is another fact, too, that constitutes a break from the divinization motif, namely, the stress on the doctrine of the Christian life and the physical coming of the Kingdom. I find that these two things contravene the more ontological presupposition with which the *Divine Principle* begins.

*Dr. Richardson:* Perhaps we have two doctrines of creation in Unification theology. Is there one articulated and stated doctrine of creation which is not a doctrine of creation at all, but a doctrine of emanation? And then do we have an implicit doctrine of creation in Unification's stress on the doctrine of the Christian life, the doctrine of the Holy Spirit and the doctrine of sin? Is it only there implicitly? Could you draw it out and put it over against the expressed and articulated doctrine of creation one finds in Section One of the *Divine Principle?*

*Farley Jones:* Maybe. But I'm not convinced that the *Divine*

*Principle* does not distinguish between the Creator and creation. Early in your paper you write, "In fact, the *Divine Principle* calls Him, God, the Universal Prime Energy." But now, in the *Divine Principle,* we read that "God is the Creator of all things. He's the absolute reality, eternally self-existent, transcendent of time and space; therefore, the fundamental energy of His Being must also be absolute and eternally self-existent. At the same time, He is the source of the energy which enables all things to maintain their existence. We call this energy (that is, the energy which enables all things to maintain their existence, which God is the source of) Universal Prime Energy." So there is, in the *Divine Principle,* a distinction between God and Universal Prime Energy.

*Dr. Vander Goot:* But the problem is right there. God is called energy, right? Even if God is distinguished from Universal Prime Energy, He is called energy. Now that is the problem. Philosophically, God is described in terms of a condition that belongs to the creation itself.

*Dr. Richardson:* But wouldn't we have to know, then, how they understand that: whether ontologically, or metaphorically, or mythically?

*Dr. Vander Goot:* You've got to take the whole context and come to a judgment on what the sense of the statement actually is. The *Divine Principle* claims that God is energy, absolute transcendent energy, although He may be distinct from Universal Prime Energy.

*Klaus Lindner:* May I add something? There is energy which enables God to create, but the energy which is created out of "give and take action" is a different energy from the energy which enables God to create. Energy is part of God's existence, but the energy out of which the universe is created is a different energy.

*Dr. Vander Goot:* But that's exactly the point. You're saying that there's something in God which finally explains the creation. There is a principle within Him, namely, energy, that finally enables Him to create Universal Prime Energy, right? That is a highly dubious conception.

*Dr. Richardson:* You mean to say that Christian teaching is that there is nothing in God that would explain how it is possible for God to create?

*Dr. Vander Goot:* There's nothing like a philosophical or metaphysical principle that would explain it, no.

*Dr. Richardson:* But the question is whether this is a philosophical or metaphysical principle or a theological mode of speaking which every Christian would use. Suppose you say, "God can create because He possesses the power to be creative."

*Dr. Vander Goot:* You're being unprincipled if you think you're explaining creation by using naive language like that. (laughter)

*Dr. Richardson:* Surely the point is that the cause has to be sufficient to produce the effect.

*Dr. Vander Goot:* God's not related to the world as cause to effect.

*Dr. Richardson:* I might say then that you're not talking any longer about Christian dogma, but that you're proposing one philosophical or theological interpretation of the Christian dogma of creation. It's perfectly clear, for example, that one type of Christian theology uses the cosmological argument, and other kinds of Christian theology argue from degrees of perfection. It may well be the case that theologians can argue whether it's right to use these arguments or not, but clearly, in the Christian tradition, these arguments are used in order to explain what it means to say that God is the Creator.

*Dr. Vander Goot:* But there's nothing uniquely Christian about that argument. That's my point. That argument was, in effect, used by the Greeks. There's nothing that differentiates the Greek conception of the relationship with God from the Christian conception.

*Dr. Richardson:* Yes, but don't you see that some Christian theologians have always thought that we had some arguments that were also used by the Greeks, and that we didn't need to make them up for ourselves. (laughter) It's an advantage. (laughter)

*Jonathan Wells:* I see a way of tying this in with our previous discussion about prayer. First of all, I'd like to say that this is a very fundamental issue and I'm not sure that any of us claim to fully understand the *Divine Principle*. But let me go back to the question of prayer. It's been my habit for the last few years, even before I was in the Church, to go out several evenings a week, usually in the mountains or the woods, to pray. I used to be quite a pantheist, and when I'd pray, I believed that my prayer was a mystical mingling with the bushes and the trees and the mountains. That's how I prayed; that's how I felt God. I think this is what you mean about confusing the Creator with the creation. I had no sense of the distinction in those days. Whereas now, when I go out and pray, as I did last night, I'm quite conscious that the trees and the rocks are the creation, and that God is quite transcendent and apart from that.

*David Jarvis:* The *Divine Principle* is operating in an Eastern philosophical mode in which it's more common to speak of God in terms of energy. I was going to say that I agree with your perception that the *Divine Principle* is saying that God in some way creates the tangible world out of Himself, out of His own energy. But I lose you at the point where you say that means that we cannot say that God is different from creation. I'd like you to clarify that distinction. Why must we choose between our ontical idea of God's creating out of His energy and our idea of God?

*Dr. Vander Goot:* Because the idea of God's creating out of His energy is not a doctrine of creation, but is really a doctrine of emanation. It seems to me that when you stress restoration as much as you do, you imply a classical doctrine of creation which cannot go hand in hand with the notion that the creation is really the external form of God who is its inner character. There's an inconsistency here.

*David Jarvis:* I don't see that. I don't even see the inconsistency of that last point.

*Dr. Vander Goot:* In the theory of emanation, restoration doesn't mean the recovery of creaturehood. It actually means freedom from creation. Man is finally reabsorbed into the Divine Being. As the creation flows from God, so it returns to Him. So whatever creation was, you restore it regardless. If you understand the created order to be an emanation of God, how can you ever have a Fall?

*Dr. Richardson:* Let's think about this in relation to the history of theology. It seems to me that in the first century of Christian theology, metaphysics, for various reasons, had not been developed in such a way that you could distinguish metaphysically between a creationist and an emanationist view of the relation between God and the world. For a thousand years of Christian theology, the way that the Church affirmed the distinction between God and the world wasn't by trying to develop a special metaphysical principle to distinguish creation from emanation, but by saying that the world had not always existed, that the world had a beginning in time. Now when you get to Anselm and St. Thomas, the philosophical arguments begin to carry the day and make a man like St. Thomas agree that one can no longer defend on philosophical grounds the doctrine that the world had its beginning in time. And so then the effort moves towards finding a distinctive metaphysical principle to distinguish between creation and emanation. So I would say that there are different ways that theology can defend the distinction between Creator and creation other than by fighting for a distinction in the metaphysical order which you call ontic distinctiveness. The most traditional way, as in Scripture and in the larger part of Christian tradition, has been to argue that the world was specially created by God, and has a distinctive beginning in time.

*Dr. Vander Goot:* My point is that within the Unification theological system itself, there is, it seems, a duality, an internal problem. There is the restoration motif on one hand and the divinization motif on the other.

*Jonathan Wells:* I still don't understand, I guess, what the problem is. In my understanding, God created the world; and then, because of the Fall, the world no longer operates in accordance with God's original wishes. I don't understand how restoration language vitiates the language of creation by failing adequately to honor the difference between God and His creation. I think that the distinction is in the *Divine Principle* because that's where I learned it. But I guess that the point is not made clear enough in the text.

*Lokesh Mazumdar:* I'd like to shift to another point. We've been talking about the *how* of creation without getting into the *why* of creation. The why can't be ignored. To carry on a discussion in this way is a very secular way of looking at God: we're not looking at the real heart, the real desire that led God to create in the way that He did. Moreover, when the *Divine Principle* talks about restoration it is not talking about changes of "energy structure," but it is talking about the restoration of love between God and His creatures. I think that that is something that needs to be pointed out.

*Dr. Vander Goot:* Well, that's why I say in my paper that this theological position cannot finally be discussed in terms of philosophical principles, but must be talked about in terms of Unification's conception of God's love. I think I have seen your point. And that is what the discussion of joy and love in my paper is about.

*Dr. Sawatsky:* I wonder if there is a prior question that underlies this discussion; and that is, can a member of the Unification Church tolerate inconsistencies or contradictions within the *Divine Principle?* Must it be systematically perfect? If it must be systematically perfect, then Henry might be uncovering its Achilles' heel. If you can tolerate variation, even inconsistencies, then you can flow with it. If, for example, we were working with Calvin's *Institutes,* we would be very concerned about consistency. If, on the other hand, we were looking at Luther's sermons, we might well come up with some contradictions and not worry about them. Even within classical Christian theology we recognize different kinds of theologizing. What are we working with here? Are we working with material that is more pastoral than systematic? That's my question.

*Tirza Shilgi:* I just wanted to say that it is generally agreed within the Unification Movement that the version of the *Divine Principle* that we have now is not the final version. Therefore, we are very interested in this kind of discussion and not very upset by it.

*Dr. Sawatsky:* That is very interesting. We are looking at a theology which itself is in the process of evolution.

*Klaus Lindner:* I don't think it's the theology itself, but the *expression* of the theology which is in the process of evolution.

*Dr. Bryant:* Well, that is a very major problem for us who are from outside. It's difficult to know what to make of the *Divine Principle.*

*Joe Stein:* I think one of the difficulties we run into is the question of emphasis. What caused me some difficulty with the paper was that something was emphasized which we don't emphasize. We place a greater emphasis on the intentional quality of God in creation. Behind the act of creation, behind the very fact of God's creating the world, lies an intention. There's a will and a desire involved. That intention is, in a sense, a form of energy which is invested. So energy doesn't become something that's material. Energy can be spiritual as well as just material. So I felt that the emphasis in this paper on the doctrine of creation didn't seem to communicate to me the essence of the doctrine of creation as it exists in the *Divine Principle.*

*Dr. Bryant:* Can you say something that may help to clarify that? What I understand you to be saying is that when you people read the *Divine Principle,* the priority is clearly on the development of a particular Unification spirituality. You want to become certain kinds of human beings, to develop a parental heart, etc. So doctrine in a formal sense is secondary to spirituality. When you say that the theology isn't changing but the expression is, it sounds like there's a basic intuition, or orientation, or sensibility that's the real stuff, and on top of that you're trying to work out a theology that is adequate to that intuition. Does that sound right?

*Joe Stein:* I think so. Just yesterday we had a talk with Rev. Moon. We discussed the question of what is primary for us: the knowledge of God, or the experience of God. And we realized among ourselves that through the experience of God, we gain knowledge and understanding; but through the mere study of God, or through an attempt to know or understand God in an external sense, we lose something. I think the experience of God is prior.

*Dr. Vander Goot:* It seems to me that Darrol's point is this: if there is a doctrine of creation, then, at least in the way it's understood, it is constructed from the retrospective glance at the doctrine of the Christian life and the doctrine of the Holy Spirit. What we have, it seems to me, in the *Divine Principle* is *that,* plus a speculative principle. You not only have a doctrine of creation constructed with a view to what you can do with it in the context of your doctrine of Christian life or doctrine of the Holy Spirit, but you also have a very speculative starting point.

*Joe Stein:* Our theology is very much based in our experience.

*Dr. Bryant:* Yes, I think that's right, but I think that what Henry is pointing out, and what seems to make people a little bit uncomfortable here, is that there is a specifically intellectual content, too, in the *Divine Principle,* that one can evaluate and consider in terms of intellectual criteria.

*David Jarvis:* Well, I'd kind of like to get back to the original question of whether or not Henry's formulation squared with what we believe. The way I see the *Divine Principle,* the doctrine of creation is committed to a certain synthesis or consonance between scientific and religious formulations of the idea of creation. And in a sense, the whole concept of energy and creation from energy has been very, very vague because science is, at this point, very vague on how that mechanism works. So we're saying that God is connected to the creation in some way, but exactly how and how this connection should be formulated we don't yet know. I think it may come more from the scientific realm through the study of the creation than through theology. Okay, that's just my guess. The how of creation, if God's the Creator, is, I think very vague at this point.

I think we're saying that God is energy, but we stress that God's energy is only one aspect of His Being. I think some of the people have brought this out. Energy is only a small aspect of God's Being. There's also intelligence, will, love, other kinds of being in God. To say that God is the creation or that we're equating God and the creation wholly is probably incorrect.

Then there's the whole question of emphasis. Because of the way the *Divine Principle* formulates the theory of creation in terms of dualities, in terms of yin and yang, you have to be very careful when you're talking about creation to specify your universe of discourse. You have to specify what system you're working through. In other words, to try and freeze it into certain rigid categories leads you into innumerable difficulties. It's a very fluid concept. Everything in the universe has these dual aspects, and when we're speaking of God it's very difficult. You have to specify the point of view that you're operating from in talking in those dualistic or dual aspect terms. However, I found your paper helpful. It made me aware of things that need to be clarified.

# WOMEN IN THE THEOLOGY OF
# THE UNIFICATION CHURCH

## *Elizabeth Clark*

Unification theology employs various myths and symbols revelatory of its attitudes toward women and sexuality, the most important of which is that of Eve's role in the Fall of humankind.
The latter topic, we may remember, was also a favorite of the
church fathers, whose comments on the subject had disturbing
consequences for the evaluation of women's position throughout
the course of western history. It is thus startling from a feminist
perspective to discover similar themes propounded in the theology
of the Unification Church. There are, however, elements both in
Unification theology itself and in the present social setting which
could militate against those symbols finding a "real-life" correlate; some aspects of the theology actually appear to temper the
otherwise misogynist and anti-sexual tone of the *Divine Principle*.
I hope the members of the Unification Church will develop these
positive themes as they concomitantly eliminate those features of
their theology which long ago and in another form contributed to
the suppression and degradation of women in western theology.
Not every church has a theology so new and flexible that it can be
reshaped when the unfortunate consequences of its presupposi-
tions are uncovered!

Unification theology follows the traditional Christian pattern
of linking the position of women with Eve's role in the Fall, and

---

All bracketed references are to the *Divine Principle,* (New York: The Holy Spirit
Association for the Unification of World Christianity, 1973, 2nd ed.) unless otherwise
noted.

combines a literal understanding of Adam and Eve as historical persons with a symbolic interpretation of some details of the Genesis account.[1] Biblical literalism is, I believe, one of the chief difficulties hampering Unification Church members in all of their theological formulations; their exegesis of the opening chapter of Genesis provides a case in point. For example, I heard from one of the Church's more thoughtful and articulate devotees about "Eve's very real emotions and experiences during the Fall. She was, after all, a human being, and not so different from you and me." Such a statement combines sheer fabrication (Eve's "emotions" are not, after all, a point on which Genesis 3 dwells) with a misunderstanding of the mythical character of the Genesis account, especially of the socially determined component of myth. Just as Genesis seeks to provide answers to such questions as "Why do we Hebrews consider the Canaanites cursed?", so it attempts to answer the query, "Why do we see all around us that men dominate women?" Biblical scholars interested in the social structures of ancient Hebrew culture would no doubt offer less ingenious and charming answers to these questions than do chapters 2 and 3 of Genesis. Just as they might note that the religious leaders of the Hebrews were for centuries involved in a fierce contest with Canaanite values and used any opportunity available to slander that culture, so likewise they could assert that Hebrew men did in fact rule over their women, and that Genesis 3 provides an explanation of how that state of affairs came to be. To interpret such myths apart from the cultural context which produced them can result in the upholding of values inappropriate to twentieth century western culture, as we shall shortly see.

Adam and Eve, according to the *Divine Principle,* should have first perfected their own individualities, then married and formed a family centered on God. [41-43] Their relationship with God would have formed a "Trinity," and as their descendants matured and married, each couple in turn would have become a "Trinity" with the Deity. [217] God's original intent for the human race was that it should be "one great family" [123] constituting the Kingdom of God here on earth. [101] The Fall, unfortunately, prevented these ideal conditions from being realized.

The essence of the Fall is given a somewhat different interpretation by Unification theologians than by traditional Christian

---

[1] pp. 66, 69. Thus the fruit of the tree in Eden was not real fruit; how could the eating of food cause original sin to be transmitted to later generations? Likewise, the two trees of the garden are not really trees, but symbolize Adam and Eve.

writers: it is sexual and is viewed as fornication, or variously, as adultery, [72, 75] first committed by Eve with the tempter arch- angel. This union is described as a "blood relationship" having both spiritual and sexual components. [77] And to those who might raise a skeptical eyebrow at the possibility of a flesh-and- blood woman mating with an archangel, the *Divine Principle* af- firms that "sexual union with a spirit is possible" and offers the near rape of Lot's two angelic visitors as a confirming example.[2]

Lucifer had a threefold motivation in occasioning the Fall: he envied God's love for Adam and Eve; [78] he was jealous that Adam was to be Eve's future husband;[3] and his desire was aroused. (Eve seemed beautiful to him because he was a member of the opposite sex, the *Divine Principle Study Guide* informs us.[4] Are we to assume that if Lucifer had had homosexual preferences, the onus of guilt for the original sin would have fallen on Adam?) Unification Church practitioners stress that Lucifer's sin was es- sentially spiritual: He followed his own desires rather than God's, attracted primarily by the radiance Eve exuded as the result of God's love of her. Although the archangel was motivated by love, his mistake lay in his misuse of that emotion.[5] Such an exegesis does much to offset the simplistic picture of Lucifer as a lusty male, desirous of sexual relations with a human female, as were the "sons of God" of Genesis 6. On the other hand, this interpre- tation is not one which uninstructed readers would necessarily de- rive from a straightforward reading of the text of the *Divine Prin- ciple.*

Eve's motivation, in contrast, was her "excessive desire to en- joy what was not yet time for her to enjoy; that is, to become like God, with her eyes opened (Gen. 3:5)." [242] This explanation is confusing. What Eve was going to enjoy later on was a sexual rela- tionship; are we to imagine that "becoming like God and having her eyes opened" also refers to her introduction to sexual experi- ence? Such an assumption implies that if our likeness to God is sexual, the Deity also engages in sexual relations. Or are we rather to revert to the traditional interpretation, that the serpent lured Eve with a promise of superior "wisdom," however that word

---

[2] p. 77. The reference is to Genesis 19:1-11.

[3] *The Divine Principle Study Guide, Part I* (Tarrytown, N.Y.: The Holy Spirit Associa- tion for the Unification of World Christianity, 1973), p. 82

[4] *Study Guide,* I, p. 83.

[5] I am indebted to Cathryn Cornish, Registrar at the Unification Theological Seminary at Barrytown, N.Y., for this interpretation.

may be interpreted, and that *this* is what "having open eyes" means? This second interpretation appears to govern the statements in the *Divine Principle* that Lucifer seemed "older and wiser" to Eve and that through her union with him she received "fear and wisdom."[6] (In any sexual relationship, according to Unification theology, we acquire the character of our partner; hence Eve in her union with Satan also "inherited" his evil nature. [89]) We are in addition given the explanation that it was because the good impulses of Eve's "original mind" were overcome by the power of "non-principled love" that she engaged in "give-and-take action" with Satan. [93-94] The *Divine Principle* is thus somewhat ambiguous as to whether Eve was impelled primarily by sexual desire or by more spiritual promptings.

Even at this point in the drama of the Fall, however, Eve could have been rescued and the horrendous consequences of the Fall avoided. [91] If Adam had not fallen and had developed his own perfection, he could have served as a mediator between Eve and God, restoring her to God's good favor[7] — a point which leads me to doubt whether Eve's sin was so terrible after all and Christians to inquire whether Adam is here being endowed with Messianic capacities of mediatorship between the divine and the human.

Eve, alas, was not rescued, but rather proceeded to seduce Adam. She is at least given credit for having had a virtuous motivation in doing so: we are told that she "wanted to go back to God's side after realizing the illicit nature of her relationship with the archangel." [80] Unification Church members emphasize that Eve was acting in ignorance of God's will for her and for Adam. She possessed so little faith that she did not even think to ask God what His plans for them might be. This rather than the sex act with Adam was the essence of her sin, they claim.[8] But however good an intention we attribute to Eve, her temptation of Adam constituted a second Fall. [241] Eve assumed the role in relation to Adam that the archangel had assumed toward her (that is, as seducer to seducee), and thus transferred to Adam in her "blood relationship" with him all the evil elements she had received from Lucifer. [80, 89]

What were the results of the Fall? First of all, Unification theology makes it clear that it was not physical but spiritual death

---

[6] *Study Guide,* I pp. 82-83.

[7] *Study Guide,* p. 84.

[8] I am indebted to Cathryn Cornish for this interpretation.

which was introduced by the Fall. [169-170] Adam would have died a physical death even if he had *not* sinned, the *Divine Principle,* following Pelagius, states. Not physical death, but the relinquishing of human beings to "Satanic dominion" was one effect of the Fall. In becoming one body with Satan, man became Satan's dwelling place, [102] and the physical transfer of original sin is the sign of Satan's rule over us. Secondly, Adam and Eve felt shame about their sexual organs, since the sinful "blood relationship" with Satan had been engaged in by means of those "lower parts." [259] Thirdly, the order of dominions was upset in the Fall: the angel who was to be dominated by man instead dominated Eve, who was supposed to be under the dominion of Adam, dominated him instead." [91] The result was a disorderly human society.

Since the original sin involved us in both physical and spiritual evil, we must await a Messiah who will redeem us not just spiritually, as Jesus did, but physically as well. [148, 511] The original sin which is transmitted through the flesh still awaits dissolution so that it is not transferred to the next generation. This step will be achieved by the Lord of the Second Advent.[9] As far as the redeeming of male dominion which had been upset by Eve's ill-conceived action, we gather that this has already occurred and is symbolized by the institution of circumcision in the Old Testament, explicitly described as "the sign of restoring male dominion." [305] The myth of the Fall thus provides one central group of images by which women and human sexuality can be understood in Unification theology.

The Fall of Eve, of course, is scarcely a new theme in western theology. Since the early days of Christianity, Eve and all women after her have been blamed for the world's sinfulness. Despite Paul's words in Romans 5 that "in *Adam* all sinned," the author of 1 Timothy (2:14), writing forty or fifty years later, claimed that "Adam was not deceived, but the woman was deceived and became a transgressor." From here it was but a short step to Tertullian's famous invective against women:

> Do you not know that each of you is also an Eve? . . . You are the devil's gateway. You are the unsealer of that forbidden tree. You are the first deserter of the divine law. You are she who persuaded him who the devil was not valiant enough to attack. You destroyed so easily God's image, man. Because of the death which you brought upon us, even the Son of God had to die.[10]

---

[9] pp. 368-369. Most Unification Church members believe that the Lord of the Second Advent will be Rev. Moon.

[10] *On the Apparel of Women,* I, 1.

It is obvious why feminists from Elizabeth Cady Stanton to Mary Daly have understood the story of the Fall to be the central destructive myth concerning women in western culture. Stanton had a simple remedy for the problem. She wrote:

> Take away the snake, the fruit-tree, the woman from tableau, and we have no fall, no frowning Judge, no Inferno, no everlasting punishment — hence no need of a Saviour. Thus the bottom falls out of the whole Christian theology.[11]

Many might object that her solution is somewhat simplistic; nonetheless, it pointedly reveals the strength of her conviction that the story of Eve has exerted a deleterious influence upon western attitudes toward women. The major motifs of the Christian religion, Stanton implies, unfold from the tale of Eve's sin, and consequently Christianity has given its support for two thousand years to the denigration of women. If I were given the opportunity to write a new theology, I surely would wish to avoid the theme of woman's culpability for bringing sin into the world!

Another disturbing point in the Unification interpretation of Genesis 3 is that it links original sin with sexual intercourse more resolutely than does mainline Christian theology. Whatever sexual overtones traditional Christianity read into (or out of) the Fall myth, it tended to see the essence of the Fall in man's pride or rebellion against God. But when the Fall *itself* is an explicitly sexual act, it becomes more difficult to redeem sexuality, despite Unification theology's glorification of marriage and children. In addition, the very literal understanding of the transfer of original sin through sexual intercourse has negative implications for human sexual relations in general. Even Augustine, the chief architect of the theory of original sin, was careful not to claim that it was sexual intercourse *per se* which caused transfer of original sin;[12] rather, it was *God* who placed the guilt of that sin on the souls of fetuses at conception. Unification theology, on the other hand, explicitly associates the transfer of original sin with sexual intercourse. But even here the Church might stress other themes; if, as Unification theologians claim, Adam and Eve were intended by God to have a sexual relation in Paradise when they were mature, sexual intercourse cannot in itself be evil.[13] This notion provides a

---

[11] *The Critic,* March 28, 1896, cited in Aileen Kraditor, *Ideas of the Woman Suffrage Movement* (Garden City: Doubleday, 1971), p. 78, n. 11.

[12] Augustine believed that Adam and Eve would have had sinless intercourse in the Garden of Eden had they not fallen. *The City of God,* XIV, 23-24.

[13] p. 94 and *Study Guide,* I, p. 129.

more positive understanding of sexual relations than does the insistence that the sex act itself is the cause of the transfer of original sin.

In addition, Unification theory teaches that in the Kingdom, children will be conceived and born without original sin, which implies that sinless conception is a theoretical possibility for the future. Traditional Christian teaching appears conservative in comparison. Augustine, for example, thought that although Adam and Eve might have brought forth sinless children in Eden had they themselves remained innocent, that possiblity is not now an option. Even regenerated Christian parents cannot but conceive their children in original sin.[14] The only way to break that chain will be for humans to stop reproducing, as we shall indeed cease to do in the Kingdom of God, according to Augustine.[15] A more encouraging view of human sexuality could emerge in Unification theology if the possibility of sinless conception were emphasized, rather than the inevitable linking of procreation with the passage of original sin.

A third point concerning which Unification theology might be criticized by feminists is its tendency to view all life, the whole created order, as dual, describable as one or the other of two types, either "male" or "female." [21] It is not just Adam and Eve as man and woman who represent the two contrasting sets of qualities; the whole universe can be so depicted. Thus God (who is masculine) is said to create the world (which is feminine) as His object. [25] Not only is the depiction of God as masculine objectionable; the subject-object distinction is equally so, for in each such polar situation the male is described as the subject and the female as the object. Eve, for example, is called the object to Adam's subject. [24] (Such phraseology calls to mind Simone de Beauvoir's discussion of woman as "the Other" in *The Second Sex*.[16]) The masculine characteristic is, furthermore, described as "positivity" and the feminine one as "negativity." [24] There is apparently no end of things to which such male-female typology can be applied. We are even told that during the Second World War, countries divided themselves into "male" and "female." (America and Germany were male, England and Japan were female, for some reason which totally eludes me!) [486]

---

[14] *On Marriage and Concupiscence,* I, 37.

[15] *The City of God,* XXII, 17.

[16] *The Second Sex,* trans. H. M. Parshley (New York: Alfred A. Knopf, 1971, 7th printing), pp. 33,48,51 and *passim.*

Since everything operates through the combination of polarities, redemption too will require the union of a male and female to restore what Adam and Eve ruined. [123] The perfect male-female relation has already been symbolized in the divine sphere by Jesus as the model male joining Himself to the female Holy Spirit; their union gives "rebirth" to mankind. [118] The Holy Spirit is further described as the "female negativity" at work on earth which counterbalances the "male positivity" of Jesus operative in the heavens. [215] Even in the Old Testament, the "male positivity" of Jesus was symbolized by the "pillar of cloud by day," whereas the "female negativity" of the Holy Spirit was represented by the "pillar of fire by night."[17]

A student of Chinese religion might remind us at this point that Unification theology has here simply adapted for its own purposes the ancient Chinese yin-yang theme, the polarity of universal forces which can be described as male or female, positive or negative, and so forth. It could be argued that the motif as it appears in Unification theology is simply a carryover from the oriental culture out of which the Church sprang.[18] But from a feminist point of view (or more precisely, from the kind of feminist viewpoint which I espouse), viewing the world as composed of polarities and calling those polarities male and female has unfortunate consequences for our attitudes toward women, for such a mode of conceptualization serves only to reinforce the essential "differentness" of the sexes and makes any approach to an androgynous vision of life virtually impossible.

Some of my contemporaries posit the view that men and women are basically *different* in their mental, emotional, and psychic natures, but that we should not on this basis assign higher value to one group of characteristics than to the other. This view can be dubbed the "different but equal" theory of sexual relations, and it is one which I find dangerously deceptive. (Just look at the consequences of that theory as it was applied to the blacks during the civil rights struggles of the 50's and 60's.) *Either* you must affirm that men and women are or can be essentially alike, if they are given identical educations and have identical social expectations placed upon them, *or* you must affirm that one differen-

---

[17] pp. 309-310. The reference is to Exodus 13:21

[18] Some Unification Church members stress that the position of "subject" and "object" can change and hence is not irrevocably tied to the distinctions of "male" and "female," respectively. I have not found any verification of that interpretation in *Divine Principle*, however.

tiating set of qualities, male or female, is superior to the other —
and I fear I know which set that inevitably turns out to be, despite
the arguments of some feminists that the supposed female characteristics are more valuable than the ones traditionally assigned to
men. The nineteenth century opponents of women's suffrage
championed the theory that women were morally superior to men,
that they were more loving, generous, virtuous, and so forth —
and hence were so ethereal and unsullied that they could not possibly be allowed to vote, sit on juries, hold public office, make the
laws which governed them, own property, or be given college educations. The "real-life" consequences of the argument that women
are morally *superior* turn out to be the very same as those of the
argument that women are *inferior* to men. It appears that the wolf
lurking under the sheep's clothing of a supposed "female superior-
ity" is the very same wolf who gobbles up unsuspecting little girls
in a more blatant expression of male supereminence. It is no com-
fort to be lulled with the assurance that you as a female are really
"superior" to men when you are going to be the wolf's dinner, in
any case! Theories advocating the essential "differentness" of the
sexes in one way or another almost always lead to a favoring of the
supposedly male province, and I suspect the same tendency is at
work in Unification theology. A theology which describes women
as "objects" to male "subjects," or as the "negativity" which
sparks men's "positivity" cannot extricate itself from the unhappy
consequences of the "different but equal" theory of the sexes.

Another point on which I question the implications of Unification theology is the prevalence of its parenting imagery. Just as
God is described as a Parent [12] so men and women are defined
by their parental roles. In fact, this appears to be the *only* understanding of marriage in Unification theology; reproduction is the
goal of the union of husband and wife. "Multiply and fill the
earth" is taken as the second blessing God pronounced on Adam
and Eve; [41, 43] their production of children was "the purpose of
God's creation." [48] With Adam and Eve's love for God and for
each other, and their children's love for them and for God, the
"four-position foundation" would have been established, [83] the
perfection of God's intent for His world. For redemption to occur,
the good parenting practices which the first couple forfeited need
to be established, for which Jesus and the Holy Spirit provide us
with a model. [118] With the Second Advent, Christ as Bride-
groom and His bride will complete the mission which was left un-
finished at the time of Jesus' death. [152] Although the saints since
the time of Pentecost have (in Paul's words) "grafted onto" their

True Parents, Jesus and the Holy Spirit, [362] physical redemption still awaits them. The Lord of the Second Advent and his bride will succeed in stopping the transfer of original sin through the flesh. [368-69, 511-12] Presumably the children of the True Parents, the Lord of the Second Advent and his bride, the embodiment of the Holy Spirit,[19] will be the sinless inheritors of the Kingdom.

Just as students of eastern religions might note the yin-yang motif in Unification theology, so they might also trace the Church's heavy stress on the family to the emphases of traditional Chinese religion. The importance of reverence for ancestors dead and parents still alive in ancient Confucianism can hardly be overstated. Filial piety, it has been said, was "the measuring stick of all behavior and of the worth of the individual."[20] Marriage was expected of everyone, and the practice of arranged marriages and society's expectations regarding the childbearing combined to ensure that nearly all members of the culture did marry and reproduce. To a significant extent, religious ritual centered on the family, the continuance of which was viewed as an ideal to which religion gave its blessing. This emphasis on reverence for the past, for ancestors, and for parents also suggests that the appeal to authority, especially to an older or past authority, would be central to the culture's values.[21]

But to whatever extent we can explain the emphasis in Unification theology on parenting and filial devotion as an end-product of Chinese religious affirmation and hence understand its historical precedents, there are certain elements pertaining to them which are disturbing to a feminist.[22] First of all, the Unification Church teaches its practitioners to become "good children" to the True Parents. Obedience of children is essential for the Kingdom, we are told,[23] and we assume that that includes adult "children" as well as juveniles. The exaltation of filial obedience is somewhat in conflict with the high evaluation of self-assertion in the western world and its assumption that adolescent rebellion is inevitable in the process of maturation. That Francis of Assisi and Martin

---

[19]Study Guide, I, p. 199.

[20]Francis L. K. Hsu, Under the Ancestor's Shadows: Chinese Culture and Personality (New York: Columbia University Press, 1948), p. 206.

[21]Ibid., pp. 103-104, 242.

[22]Some of the more enlightened members of the Unification Church are willing to admit that certain attitudes in the Divine Principle concerning the identification of women with the family unit are not in keeping with contemporary American values and urge Unification women not to "take a giant step backward," as one of them expressed it.

[23]Study Guide, I, p. 65.

Luther, whose individual geniuses emerged only through rebellion against parents, are spiritual heroes of western civilization is no accident.

Women in our culture, however, have traditionally been strapped by a double demand for obedience, not only from older authorities, but from members of the male sex of their own age. The image of woman as a child who passes from the hand of her father to that of her husband is one against which western women have been struggling for the past two centuries, and it appears to be a retrograde action for women to accept docile roles as well-behaved obedient "children." If the exaltation of obedience as a virtue is somewhat out of keeping with the values of our society for men, it is at present a most unfortunate characteristic to laud before women.

A second bothersome aspect of the family and parenting stress in Unification theology is that presumably the only route open to members of the Church is to marry and become parents, a pattern of life somewhat at variance with the new interests of women in assuming non-maternal roles or embarking upon motherhood in such a way that they are not defined as individuals by their functions as wives and mothers. That the rejection of marriage does not seem to be an option for Unification women strikes me as unfortunate, comparable to Luther's insistence that everyone should marry.[24] (Catholicism at least gave everyone a choice!) Unification women would do well to reconsider and perhaps redefine their Church's attitudes on this point.

Let us turn now to the positive elements in Unification theology which could be developed to create a more supportive image of women. The first and probably the most important aspect of the Church's teaching in this regard is that God's first blessing on Adam and Eve was the command to develop his or her own individuality, so that body and mind should be brought into harmony [41, 43] and the "perfect goodness" of each would have been cultivated. [101] Adam and Eve, according to the Unification theology, were still in their "growth period" in Eden and had not yet achieved adult maturity, [79] so that the sexual relationship which was the occasion for the Fall occurred prematurely. Their own perfection should have been established before they entered into a love relationship with each other and conceived children, [82-83] and this is precisely what they failed to do.

---

[24] *The Estate of Marriage*, I.

It is not at all evident that the *Divine Principle* and I would agree on what "developing individuality," particularly women's individuality, might mean; I am suspicious when that theology informs me that Eve was supposed to be under the domination of Adam as part of God's good created order [91] — a view, incidentally, which is not in accordance with the texts of either Genesis 1 or 2.[25] But whatever the original intent of the phrase concerning individuality in the *Divine Principle,* here is one element of Unification theology which could be helpful to the Church's women in the affirmation of their own rights and status.

I do not, however, particularly favor the implication that the cultivation of individuality is the *first* stage in human development, after which a person passes on to marriage and childrearing, as Unification theology tends to suggest. Just as promoting a young woman's individuality should not be taken to mean, first and foremost, her preparation for motherhood, so the blessing regarding individuality should not be interpreted to imply that a person's development grinds to a halt once marriage is undertaken. In fact, marriage is the very stage of life in which the continuation of individual development is vitally important for a woman, so that husband and children do not engulf her life and define her personhood for her. That each individual should strive to become all he or she can be is a noble aspiration and one which could merit even more consideration by members of the Unification Church.

Secondly, Unification theology proclaims that the individuality which God intended for us to develop has found its social correlate in the liberation movements of the present age. The fact that slaves have been freed, that minority groups have been welcomed (albeit sometimes grudgingly!) into the mainstream of society, and that equality of the sexes has been acclaimed is in Unification theology a positive sign that the Last Days are nigh and that fallen humans are entering upon "a new age, in which they will restore God's first blessing to men," [121] that is, the blessing of the perfection of our individuality. This resounding affirmation of liberation for the oppressed and the praise of the democratic ideals which make such liberation possible could be further emphasized to the obvious benefit of Unification women.

Thirdly, the theme of the Unification Church as itself a family could, I think, be liberating for women. Throughout Christian

---

[25] In Genesis 3, Adam is given dominion over Eve as part of her punishment for sinning — and Christians might well assume that with the coming of Jesus, the effects of original sin had been largely undone, including the male domination of the female.

history, the family metaphor has served to liberate devotees of the faith from the confines of blood-kinship families and of status quo living arrangements in general. The "family" can well mean a community of like-minded persons who on the basis of a common ideology renounce more traditional lifestyles in order to devote themselves to ideals above and beyond the ones engendered by kin, race, and nation. The early Christians, for example, seemed to conceive their devotion to the new religion in family terms; they called one another father, mother, sister, and brother (to the horror of outsiders who looked askance at the implications of such language), and thereby they created a society which transcended the constraints of clan and family in the ordinary sense. Monasticism was another way in which Christianity broke the family tie and created a new "family," and I am prepared to argue that it was indeed a beneficial development for women. Centuries later, we find John Humphrey Noyes' Oneida Community freeing women from the usual ties of family life on the basis of the principle of universal love advocated by the Christian religion.[26]

Unification Church members have told me that there are at present husbands and wives living apart, and children in the community being raised by adults other than their natural parents. In addition, the nuclear family is not the projected goal for personal relationships, they claim; rather, it is envisaged that trinities of couples may live and raise their children together in a variation of the extended family system. All of these developments are encouraging, since they could be more liberating for women than the nuclear family arrangement sanctioned by our culture. I hope in general that Unification Church members will courageously attempt to live by these positive aspects of their vision and not relapse into traditional patterns of relationship which are proving themselves to be increasingly unsatisfactory for young women.

## DISCUSSION II

*Dr. Richardson:* I'll begin. Is it the case that family and marriage is what is preeminent in Unification theology? There is a three-fold blessing: perfection of individuality, and then marriage

---

[26] See Elizabeth Clark and Herbert Richardson, eds., *Women and Religion: A Feminist Sourcebook of Christian Thought* (New York: Harper and Row, 1977), pp. 191-205 for a discussion of Noyes' views concerning women and some representative texts from his writings on the subject.

and children, and then dominion over creation. It seems to me that the whole logic of the theology calls for people to grow beyond marriage and the family into the larger task of exercising dominion over creation. I had a conversation with someone else in the Unification Church who stressed this as the mark of the Kingdom: a more righteous world, government, economic order, etc. It does seem to me that there's a social value that's higher than marriage and the family.

*Linda Mitchell:* At least the second blessing has to be seen in relation to the first and third blessing. There is also something else that is very important. The concepts that we have of marriage today don't necessarily apply to the concepts in the *Divine Principle.* According to the *Divine Principle* man and woman equally take responsibility for the raising of children. So just as a man can be freed to fulfill himself as an individual, so a woman, too, fulfills herself as an individual and as a mother, and then also in the world. The entire universe is an extended family, so you're not closed into a nuclear family, but you're involved with the entire world.

*Betsy Jones:* I want to respond to your notion that right now we are in an emergency situation after which everybody will settle down to a regular type of existence. In my own case, my family and I have gone through periods of separation from each other. That's partly because it's an emergency time. But I also know that it's been a liberating experience of finding myself, finding my own value, having a freer attitude towards my children. I hope I will see it not just as an emergency measure, but as an internal training experience so that I can live together with and also live freely within my family. And I hope when we are more settled that we will not be settled in the sense of closed in, but with the vision of families living for the sake of the whole as well as fulfilling their family responsibilities.

*Diana Muxworthy:* The Unification Church views marriage like a small society. A husband and wife are not just husband and wife, but they're also friends. In this way, it's like a small society. I think that Unification marriage contributes to women's restoration.

*Dr. Clark:* I can see that.

*Lloyd Eby:* May I talk a bit about my personal experience? In 1970 I marched in the women's parade in New York. (laughter) Then, when I first heard the *Divine Principle,* I heard the Principle of Creation and I felt good about that. Then I heard the story of the Fall. It made me enormously angry, because it seemed to me that the same mistakes were being made as you were talking about in the first part of your paper. As time went on, I began to see that those distortions had come about because people have been blaming the opposite sex. In other words, it seems to me that much of the feminist movement is a way of saying, "Man, you did it." And much of male chauvinism is a way of saying to women, "You're the one who is responsible." Within the Unification Church, in the process of restoration, the focus is on saying "I'm the one that's responsible." And once one takes that view, then rather than blaming women or blaming men, there's enough blame to go around for everybody. (laughter)

*Dr. Clark:* I would agree with that view if we were already involved in a society where all children, regardless of sex, were brought up in the same way and given the same expectations and opportunities. However, I think it's harder to say that when we live in a society that has been unequal and unjust.

*Lokesh Mazumdar:* I agree with you that society is unequal and unjust. I think we would see our responsibility as building a society in which that injustice does not exist. Then, within that society, you can begin talking about relationships between men and women and families in ways that are not coercive or destructive, but rather creative.

*Dr. Clark:* I suppose my question is exactly the one raised earlier. I see you are trying to build a new society. But what are you going to do about the *Divine Principle?* Are you going to do a different version of the *Divine Principle* so it doesn't contain these elements I'm talking about?

*Dr. Richardson:* I don't think that the *Divine Principle* describes Adam as having dominion over Eve, or that he is to be her lord. One has to read those texts in the light of what they mean, and the determining categories are these: subject-object, positivity-negativity, and most important, because most concrete, give-and-take. Now, it seems to me that if I were to try to make the argument that the Unification people are trying to make, it would run something like this. What is wrong with the Christian thinking that the man has dominion over the woman is that there can be no give-and-take relationship where one party is subservient to the other. Give-and-take can only take place where there is equality between parties. Now, a certain kind of an American abstract individualism is interested in equality between parties, where the Unification Church is concerned about the creative process, the creative interaction between the parties. And for creative interaction between the parties, there does have to be that which simple justice requires, namely, equality; but there also has to be a kind of difference. Now, when we say the difference is positivity-negativity, give-and-take or subject and object, we don't say that those roles remain always the same. Sometimes the male is subject, and sometimes the woman is subject, and when you give-and-take, the one who receives also gives. So what we're concerned about then is a creative process or interaction between the two parties. Now, to have that, it works out like this. Both parties can't be talking at the same time; someone has to be listening while somebody else is talking. If you want the other party to talk, you have to stop talking and listen, so that they can talk. Essentially, the relationship between man and woman should be a model for every relationship in the sense that equality and difference facilitates process. I think that's the view of the Unification Church.

*Dr. Clark:* But there's absolutely nothing built into that scheme that has anything to do with men and women, insofar as every single human being is a different individual. Two men could have this relationship and two women could have it, etc. Why do we have to divide it into male and female? It's loaded.

*Dr. Richardson:* Unification holds the view that masculinity is in women and femininity is in men when women act as subject and men act as object. And I would take it that the categories masculinity and femininity are not the same as male and female, but refer to that capacity in either or anyone to play the role of subject or object. Essentially, then, there is the definition of biology in terms of a spiritual range of concepts rather than the other way around. And I suppose a kind of a sophisticated argument would say that the biological difference is only to remind us of the spiritual difference, and we shouldn't get trapped by it. You have to realize that the focus is not, as Lloyd was saying, on who's to blame, or who more than the other; but the focus is this very practical problem, namely, how you get something going with another person is by finding a point of interaction and access, and that's what this language is about, I think.

*Jonathan Wells:* We've all heard Rev. Moon talk about this point often, and I think it's important to distinguish between the word "dominion" and the word "domineering." When Rev. Moon talks to us about marriage, he never tells the men how to keep their wives under their thumbs. (laughter) It's never like that at all. Instead, he says that the essence of marriage is living your life for the sake of your spouse, and sacrificing yourself completely for your wife, or for your husband. The spirit is constantly the spirit of self-sacrifice and humility, and never of domination.

*Dr. Clark:* I would say that, in itself, is very unfortunate for women. I feel very differently about men. Men can be nice, filial, obedient children. That's fine with me. They can be humble, patient, self-sacrificing; that will do a lot of men a great deal of good. But I think that for women to be told to be humble and self-sacrificing is destructive: that's what women have had to be for thousands of years. They ought to get out of being humble and self-sacrificing.

*Lokesh Mazumdar:* May I say something about this? There are two aspects that one needs to look at. One is the ideal state of affairs that should have been but wasn't because of the Fall. The other is things as they are in a context of restoration. The archangel took Eve away first, from God, and second, from her future husband, her potential mate. So, in a sense, the archangel dominated the relationship that Adam and Eve had, so, in a sense, he dominated both Eve and Adam. Now man has that archangel's nature and seeks to dominate women. In the restoration context, you will see a reversal of all these things, with the woman leading the way to God. We see that the task of the woman is to break away from domination, from the influence of the archangel, or of man, and to move towards an unwavering relationship with God. Then man, who has been captivated by woman, will follow. This is the way the restoration takes place. Without Eve leading the way to God, there can be no restoration.

*Dr. Clark:* Is that going to be written into the *Divine Principle?*

*Lokesh Mazumdar:* It is written into it. There's a sequel to what I said. I think the subject-object relationship that we see enacted in the fallen world may not be true to the way things were actually meant to be. I think that once the restoration is accomplished up to a certain level, then the real significance and the real meaning of subject-object relationships will probably get worked out. Then we will have something different from what we have today.

*Dr. Sawatsky:* I want to raise one question that we have missed so far. And then I want to come back to the same discussion. In the eschatology of Unification, there's a differentiation made between democratic countries and regimes and ideologies and more authoritarian and communistic structures. God is obviously on the side of the democratic countries and structures: salvation is not individualistic, salvation is communal. So I think what you're looking for from a feminist perspective will not work here. I think it's obvious that it won't work, simply because a fulfilled person is always in relationship with somebody else. Unification salvation is communal. You have to have a relationship, you have to have give-and-take. That's essential in salvation.

*Dr. Clark:* What I object to in Unification theology is the heavy stress on the one man, one woman tie as the model of mutual support, rather than the notion that people of different sexes can relate to each other and give to each other support and strength without necessarily tying that community support to a nuclear family pattern.

*Dr. Bryant:* It seems to me that you take some of the language of subject-object, masculinity-femininity and see problems in it that do not respect some careful definitions of these terms within the text. Masculinity-femininity are not just general terms, but are identified with certain qualities which are specified. It seems to me that there's a prior assumption of the meaning of these terms in your paper. This allows you to assume that if they use this kind of language, certain consequences are more or less inevitable. You assume that these concepts have such fixed consequences that they inevitably work themselves out in a community in a specific way. I wonder about that. Sometimes when I read the *Divine Principle* I find myself objecting to the language. And then I try to figure out what the language means in the context. It isn't always the language I would choose, but at least I find that it is more carefully used than I thought on first reading.

*Dr. Clark:* The language has been so loaded for so many centuries! Reading it probably doesn't strike you with the same malaise as it strikes me. To me, it's as if you were saying that we're all really equal in terms of race and so on, but then went on to talk about niggers and kikes! It's as if the Unification people were asking us to erase from our minds all the negative associations those words have had and to think of them in a new and positive way. There are lots of other ways of talking which avoid that kind of loaded language. If you don't mean by those words the kind of connotation they've carried historically, well, then, find other words. So many of you have said, "Well, we don't mean *that,* what we really mean is something else." Okay, express the "something else" rather than use terms which buy into centuries and centuries of bad associations.

*Dr. Richardson:* The problem is that this language is in the Bible, so any religion that works with the Bible is stuck with this destructive language. And I think there's no question about its being destructive. As a practical problem, it's a difficult matter to know how the Unification Church could get rid of this language and put it another way. How could any Christian church get rid of that language? It would seem to me that the way to get out of the language is to invoke the Completed Testament. Unification is a religion that's going to deal with three states, and systematically I suppose one can argue that the language of creation in the Old Testament is going to have to be qualified by the language describing man and woman in the Completed Testament. I think there's some reason to say that a kind of male-female dual Messiah is a help here. I think it's a help also to have equality between the husband and the wife. And then, of course, what would really help would be to develop a social institution which would embody these things, so that when someone said, "Hey, but you have this Old Testament dominion stuff" you could say, "Well, we have to interpret that in the light of what we actually do and have and are." I think that if one could do that, that's the best that any Christian church can do. I don't know what anybody can do, because as you know, the dominion language isn't just in Genesis, it's all through the Old Testament. You have concubines, polygamy, the slaughter of wives to assuage enemies, etc. I don't know what Christianity can do about this stuff. It's in there, but hermeneutically speaking, the text is not written with a view to propagating these theories.

*Lloyd Eby:* I very much agree with Dr. Richardson. First of all, one of the things that obviously needs restoring is language itself. One of the results of the Fall is that language itself has been debased. I agree with you that it's unfortunate that some of these terms we use have a history of bad connotations; but if one can take this language and use it in a way that reinterprets it for what we would call restored meaning, I think that's a step toward restoring language.

The second thing I want to say is that in the practice within the Unification Church as compared to religious societies in the past, I think we've gone some distance toward working out some of the problems between men and women. I know, for example, that the first missionary to the United States from Korea was a woman. I know that in the past the Church leaders in some countries have been women. When I came into the Unification Church the person from whom I learned the most in the first six months was a woman, a woman who's now the wife of one of the Seminary students. The director of perhaps the largest and most active Unification Church Center in America is a woman. These are just some of the examples of women who have had positions of responsibility in the Church. So, it seems to me that we've gone some distance toward restoring two things: restoring language, and restoring relationships.

*Dr. Clark:* I can see something of the restored relationships. But I doubt whether the language can at this point be restored. We're too close in time to the negative use of the language. You can't just use a word which has had a negative association and claim that now it has a positive use. It probably isn't going to work.

*Dr. John Kuykendall:* What do the women seminarians see before them as vocational possibilities? Do you see the same opportunities, prospects, and challenges as the men going through the seminary with you?

*Diana Muxworthy:* I say yes. There are some other things I'd like to say, but I'll just answer that and let some other people answer.

*Dr. Clark:* Can I ask you, then, how you think your family life is going to work with your role as Church leaders? As a very practical kind of project, how are you going to get it together? It's one thing to say you *will,* and another thing to do it, which, I guess, is what I'm interested in.

*Diana Muxworthy:* I would say I could do it, and it's just up to me to do it. The Church is not standing in the way of my doing it. I only stand in the way of whether I do it or not. And the *Divine Principle* is certainly not standing in the way of my doing it.

*Dr. Kuykendall:* Could you live with a "house husband?" Could you maintain your ministerial office and allow your husband to take care of the necessities of home and the small children?

*Diana Muxworthy:* I would like to answer that in terms of my own personal relationship with the *Divine Principle.* Within feminism the issue — correct me if I'm wrong — has to do with the woman's and man's functions: woman as mother, woman as housewife and husband as moneymaker and all that kind of thing. I don't think in those terms, and I don't really think the *Divine Principle,* at least for me, has anything to do with that way of defining the issue. To me, the *Divine Principle* has much more to do with an internal understanding of my relationship to my husband, whether I have a job or whether I am a mother doing dishes. The value is not in doing dishes or having a job; the value is in the depth of the relationship with that husband, but not in the function that I have. In other words, I don't think of the *Divine Principle* as defining external roles, which I think is what a lot of feminism does. The value that is given to cleaning dishes as compared to the value of the president of General Motors isn't something I worry about. I think that will all be taken care of. The real question is the internal one: how the individual person is involved in the application of the *Divine Principle.* Those practical matters will be taken care of if the divine principle is fulfilled in the internal connection that the individual people and that marriage have with God.

*Linda Mitchell:* There is something else that's important. I think that there are many men who enjoy cooking, and I think that because in the past this has been a job given to women, it's been degraded. But there's nothing that's unfulfilling about cooking, nor is there anything unfulfilling about childrearing. I think that each individual, whether a man or a woman, has a certain character and a certain personality to fulfill, be they male or female. I think that how a male or a female ultimately fulfills himself or herself depends not on his sex, but on his personality. I see this being more freely accomplished in the Unification Church because we're free to want to be a child-raiser and to take care of a home if that's what fulfills the individual. And we're free to do something else, if that's what is needed for fulfillment.

*Tirza Shilgi:* I have a feeling that one of the essential points is not exactly what the people would do with the kitchen work, but how it is that we will be able to achieve harmony between two people in the same way that things in nature, for example, exist in harmony. I think in different cases we need to do things a different way. There's something very interesting about the Church in Japan, for example. Our women in the Church are far more outgoing and active than the normal Japanese women. They're very shy, and our Church women are far more aggressive than the Japanese women. What I feel is that harmony means bringing things where they are trying to lead themselves. If it requires a woman to become more outgoing, then that's what she should do. And if in another case there's something else which is needed, then that should be done. I think that everything is guiding itself to the point of original harmony that was supposed to be there. And it would take different ways in different countries, and different aspects in individual cases.

*Dr. Kuykendall:* Can I ask a sociological question? Are there more females than males in the Church in the Orient?

*Tirza Shilgi:* I think it's pretty equal all around the world.

*Dr. Kuykendall:* Many Protestant churches in Japan have more females than males. The usual characteristics have been that the females in the churches in the Orient are more liberal than their cultural counterparts.

*Christa Dabeck:* I think that in the beginning of our Church, there were more women in the Oriental countries, but now, it's balanced.

I agree with what Linda says: the main thing is to become a person, and to achieve individual maturity. This is really what is stressed in Unification theology. I would say that there doesn't exist a picture of how a woman should be, or how a man should be. And the second point I want to make is about the practical matters. I think that we can be more flexible in fulfilling different functions because of our mutual relations. Life in the Unification Church is meant to develop the capacities of men and women for mature love — that is what we are working for.

# THE UNIFICATION CHURCH:
## SOME PRELIMINARY SUGGESTIONS
## FOR HISTORICAL AND
## SOCIAL SCIENTIFIC ANALYSIS

*Rodney Sawatsky*

Critical analyses of the Unification Church from historical or social scientific perspectives are, as yet, limited. To develop the necessary data for such analyses "field studies," alongside other methodologies, are imperative. This essay is a preliminary report of one such study which took the form of a series of conversations with a community of Unification devotees at their seminary in Barrytown, New York.

## Two Dominant Impressions

Two impressions of the Unification phenomenon prove dominant and premise all successive observations. For one, the Unification devotees or "Moonies," as they willingly refer to themselves, present an aura of quiet confidence in the rightness and ultimate triumph of their cause, which impresses one as an unusual "healthy-mindedness." Secondly, the confluence of many typically American motifs in this new religion should result in great interest in Unification among students of American religion; while its nuanced understanding of classic religious questions, solutions to these problems, and its evolutionary hermeneutic (read also, still not fully formulated!) should fascinate all students of religion.

The dangerously slippery category of "healthy-mindedness" is used here, following William James' direction, to characterize a battery of items both psychological and theological. Note for example that over half of the faculty teaching at the Unification Seminary are non-Moonies — they are Jewish, Presbyterian, Orthodox, etc.; that a number of Unification scholars will be pursuing Ph.D. work in Religion at major American and foreign universities; that open-ended, critical dialogue such as was experienced in our seminar is not threatening although evidently chastening to the believers; that doctrinal variation (fundamentalist or modernist?) openly coexist without seemingly undermining the community's cohesion; that insiders share their autobiographies with each other and with (selected) outsiders with appropriate modesty but without fear of being hurt; that despite the sinfulness of illicit or premature sexual activity, men and women devotees mingle freely and comfortably, and that our group at least found Moonies engaging and delightful associates.

Such a mood of openness is especially interesting since youthful movements with young converts are typically defensive, separatist, and insecure, most notably with reference to the educational institutions of the dominant culture. Possibly, less obvious defense mechanisms serve to shield the converts from the relativizing influences of the "outside" world. The highly disciplined and centrally controlled community known as "The Family" in which all American Moonies live may well provide a mechanism sufficient to allow considerable intellectual freedom. Furthermore, since the prophet and potential Messiah, Rev. Moon, is still alive, a charismatic focus of faith still prevails, rather than a more rigid, institutionalized authority.

Unification theology undoubtedly contributes to this mood of quiet confidence. According to James, "healthy-mindedness is a tendency which looks on all things and sees that they are good,"* and Unification thought supplies the needed theology for such ends. Sin is real, but can readily be vanquished by good. Optimism prevails regarding the human potential not only for good, but for God-like perfection. The Kingdom will come on earth imminently, first in Korea, then likely in America, and as communism is defeated, to the ends of the earth. Edenic man, the center of the Unification theology, will be restored just as soon as perfect parents populate the world with perfect offspring. American millenarianism in a Social Gospel idiom lives in Unification

---

*Wm. James, *The Varieties of Religious Experience* (New York, New York: Collier Books, 1961), p. 85.

thought. Such an optimistic world view, in James' "liberal" perspective, yields healthy-minded religious folk — and the Moonies qualify.

## Both a Sect and a Movement

Further suggestions as to the unique versus typical character-istics of Unification vis-a-vis more general American religious pat-terns may be noted as Unification is characterized as being primar-ily a movement, but is also evidencing signs of a sect.

Sectarian elements, given the definitions offered by Ernst Troeltsch and Bryan Wilson, can definitely be located in Unifica-tion. Induction into the group, for example, assumes a conversion to the truth of the *Divine Principle*. The nature of this conversion, as in traditional Christianity, may vary in emotional intensity and intellectual rigor, but it does separate the faithful theologically. Sociologically, separation follows as the new devotees move into a communal life-style. Personal wealth and personal decision-mak-ing are shared in a semi-Hutterian fashion. Jobs and education (ordinarily) are abandoned to devote full time to the propagation of the faith and the cultivation of personal perfection. Modesty in apparel and appearance further may distinguish the true believers from the rest of society.

Other theological factors may also be considered to be sec-tarian in that they represent a "protest" or at least a deviation from dominant religious perspectives. Authority in Unification is attributed to Rev. Moon, who has articulated his message and mis-sion in a theological interpretation of the Christian Scriptures known as the *Divine Principle*. Moon is perceived as the Third Adam, the Messiah for the final days, although his ultimate role in God's providence depends somewhat on his fulfillment of his potentialities. Moon is the center of the new religion; he operates in a theocratic fashion, and serves as a cult figure. He is the object of great adoration, if not always of actual worship.

The salvation offered by Unification comes via the comple-tion to perfection of the family. Parents loving each other and God perfectly will, in turn, produce perfect children — and the King-dom will be in progress. Although a new appreciation for the sanc-tity and pre-eminence of the family may not be anti-American, the highlighting of this institution to play a salvific role surely is a pro-test against the current state of the family in America and abroad.

The nation stands alongside the family as a primary institution in God's providence. Democracy is godly, and democratic nations are on God's side. Totalitarian nations because they are materialistic and anti-religious must be vanquished, preferably by the spirit but if necesssary also by the sword, before the Kingdom can come. Human history can be understood and predicted through a typological understanding of Biblical symbols and chronology. On the basis of such evidence the evolution of mankind is indeed progressing onward and upward. Biblical dating and the "signs of the times" point to Rev. Moon as the returned Messiah, and indicate impending utopia, not apocalyptic chaos. Yet, resignation is not legitimate; rather God-fearing families and nations must actively assist in channeling history to its inevitable goal. Hence, financial and political power are important for the movement to assure the right direction of history.

Characteristics such as these may convince scholars such as Bryan Wilson that Unification is a "revolutionist" sect. But the category of "sect" does not do justice to all the above data, and cannot contain some other aspects of Unification. It may be helpful to see some other aspects of Unification. It may also be helpful to see Unification as another form of *The Kingdom of God in America* motif or movement as described by H. Richard Niebuhr.

Sectarianism, typically, is defined as appealing to the dispossessed. Although Unification membership is youthful, with an average age in the mid-twenties, no ready pattern can be ascertained to characterize the devotees. Educational, social, or financial deprivation would be true of some but not of a majority of Moonies. If Unification devotees are to be typified, other than dispossession or deprivation categories will almost assuredly need to be used.

In Troeltsch's classical categories at least, sectarianism assumes the formation of an alternative community of faith which is the new vehicle of redemption. Unification proposes no new institutions, no new church. Present Unification structures are only of interim, pragmatic value but have no long term role. Salvation comes through existing organizations — namely, the family and the nation. Religious denominations also play their legitimate functions and Moonies participate in the ministrations of various Christian and non-Christian groups. But these varied religious groups serve to strengthen the individual, the family and the nation; they are not organisms in their own right which in God's providence may contradict and supersede the nation, or even the family. Unification thus is less an institutional entity than a dynamic directing existing institutions to their rightful task.

Salvation, thus, in Unification thought does not necessarily require becoming a member of the organization. Indeed, redemption, which is almost invariably the central doctrine of sectarianism, is secondary to creation, a doctrine typically more characteristic of a *corpus Christianum* or "churchly" perspective. Unification propounds a cosmology which affirms a great variety of created orders — political, economic, scientific, artistic, etc. — and does not eschew these as part of an evil world. Redemption is simply a matter of directing all of creation to its rightful destiny. Accordingly, when one correctly understands the purposes of creation and willfully acts accordingly, he is saved — in or out of Unification — although one who has eyes to see surely will join the movement.

Unification thus may be seen as keying into several movements in American religion as much as being a new sect. Rather than being separatist, in its inclusivism Unification shares in various ecumenical or possibly civil religion movements in America. By working through existing institutions it is another of many renewal movements. In its relating of sin to sexuality, in its perfectionism, and its communalism, it finds much in common with American utopian movements. In its reading of history to argue that America has a unique role in God's providential purposes, it finds much in common with American millennial and Kingdom of God themes.

Despite its being as much movement oriented as sectarian, the inexorable tendency will be for Unification to become just another denomination. Institutions once developed create their own rationale for permanence. The pragmatic function of Unification institutions surely will give way to typical denominational organization. This judgment is not necessarily predicated on the predictive inaccuracy of Unification regarding the imminent Kingdom, but rather on the refusal of other religious groups to accept this new revelation, which in turn will inevitably force Unification into being a separate group to nurture its faith despite rejection.

### Questions on Perfection

The recurrent perfectionist theme in the above paragraphs deserves a separate word regarding its sociological implications. It will be remembered that the Kingdom comes through perfected parents producing perfected offspring.

Rev. and Mrs. Moon's children apparently are to be the first fruits in the perfected order. If these children are necessarily more perfect or of a different order than the children of other perfected Unification parents is unclear. At any rate, the test of the truth of Unification or at least its potential for truth is in the very offspring now being born. Here is a category of verification not unlike the return of the Lord in 1843.

What happens if these children follow the way of all children heretofore? Will Unification need to readjust its requirements for perfection even as dates have been postponed in apocalyptic cults? Such questions are most interesting, and others follow. For example, the Unification notion of the origin of sin is more genetic than environmental. What are the indicators of a genetically perfect child? Does perfect *agape* mean sinlessness?

The sociology of marriage which assists this perfectionism is likewise interesting. Marriages, for one, are arranged, thus running counter to the tradition of romantic love of modern Western marriages. Furthermore, marriages are not consummated until the couple reaches sufficient perfection. During this pre-consummation period couples typically live apart until the movement determines they are prepared to have the perfect children.

Rev. Moon is central to this entire perfectionism. He has fathered the first fruits of the millennium, he chooses marriage mates, he marries and blesses the couples. The questions then follow: Is Rev. Moon's history and life-style critical for the movement? What might studies in the "life of Moon" do for or against the movement? What happens when Rev. Moon dies? Is there a process of succession? Or in other words, what happens when the charisma is routinized?

Because the anticipated perfection is still to come, obviously more questions remain than are answered, probably not only for the outsider but for the insider alike. These questions and observations, however, are some of the data which need to be considered in historical and social scientific analyses of the Unification Church.


## An Afterword


A brief visit to the Unification Church in Berkeley, California indicates that significant variations exist between the eastern and western wings of the American Unification body. Since the above paragraphs are based exclusively on studies of the "Moonies" at the Barrytown seminary in New York, qualifications would be necessary on some matters to have this analysis apply equally to the Unification Church in all geographical regions of America and the world.

## DISCUSSION III

*Lloyd Eby:* I think it's true that the kind of optimism that you're referring to is part of Unificationism. But maybe you have overemphasized it. There's definitely the view that the Kingdom is coming, but I think we would be naive if we think it's going to be tomorrow or this afternoon or this evening. The time period is open to question. I remember Rev. Moon saying that there comes a time when winter is past and spring is here, but precisely when that time is, you don't know.

*Dr. Sawatsky:* In something I read, someone raised with Dr. Kim the question of what would happen if Moon died. She said that Jesus didn't have a physical resurrection, but a spiritual resurrection, and implied that maybe Rev. Moon would rise again spiritually. Are you saying that the timeframe may not come within the lifetime of Rev. Moon, but somehow or other he might still have some kind of spiritual effect on people after he dies?

*Lloyd Eby:* Whether the Kingdom comes or not, I think he would have a spiritual effect on people after he dies.

*Dr. Sawatsky:* But you don't see the precipitation of the Kingdom as necessarily prior to his death?

*Lloyd Eby:* Yes, I would say that prior to his death certain things have to be accomplished. And once those things are accomplished, then the momentum will be overwhelming.

*Dr. Sawatsky:* What specific things?

*Lloyd Eby:* I think the important thing is that a number of families have to be established. I think probably that's the most important.

Also, you say in your paper that "The Kingdom will come on earth imminently, first in South Korea, then in America, and as communism is defeated, to the ends of the earth." I think it remains to be seen where the Kingdom will first be set up substantially. It will probably be in South Korea, but I don't think that it necessarily has to be there.

*Farley Jones:* As long as we're on that topic, I have a question. It seems to me that the implication of the *Divine Principle* is that the Kingdom wouldn't come just in South Korea, but that it would be in Korea through the unification of South and North.

Unification is central to the whole task of establishing the Kingdom. The second point is that I don't think that America is necessarily the second place where the Kingdom's going to come. I don't see a necessary sequence. I don't think it's clear to any of us at this point what the whole sequence is going to be or how it's supposed to happen. The third point concerns phraseology. Why say that the Kingdom will come? That way of saying it removes it from man's responsibility. Rev. Moon emphasizes that we have to build the Kingdom with our own hands. I think if we use language like "the Kingdom will come," it brings forth images of something floating down from the sky. That's not how we see it at all.

*Lloyd Eby:* You also say that "Authority in Unification is attributed to the Bible plus a theological interpretation of the Christian Scriptures known as the *Divine Principle* . . . ." That's true, but there's something about that that makes me uneasy. I think we would say that the primary source of authority is the man who occupies the position of Messiah, and that, as Jesus made clear, it was the Scriptures that testified to Him, not his testifying to the Scriptures. In other words, Jesus made clear that He was the authority, and that it was through Him that the Scriptures could be interpreted. So primary authority would rest with the man, not the writings, although that is not to deny authority to writings.

*Dr. Sawatsky:* This talk about authority is helpful. I've been sensing today that authority is much more the man than the written documents. That, I think, has become more obvious than it was to me the last time we were here. This makes the question of what happens when the man is no longer with us more acute.

*Lloyd Eby:* Something else has to be said about that. There's a sense in which one can say that Rev. Moon has authority because he is the embodiment of the divine principle. In other words, the divine principle itself is something different from what's written in the Black Book. It's the Principle through which God has operated in nature and time.

*Dr. Sawatsky:* Just as conventional Christians could talk about the Word and the word?

*Lloyd Eby:* Right. The Black Book says something to the effect that it is an expression of the truth, not the truth itself.

*Dr. Clark:* Are you going to answer the other part of the question? What happens when the living Word passes from the scene? Do we then have to depend upon the written word?

*Lloyd Eby:* My understanding of what happens when the living Word passes from the scene is that, in fact, the living Word does not pass from the scene. It passes from the scene only physically.

*Dr. Clark:* But remains as the spirit?

*Lloyd Eby:* Yes. Just as at the time of Pentecost, the disciples of Jesus had some kind of spiritual connection with Him.

*Dr. Bryant:* Is that right? I thought that the point of Unification was the completion of the spiritual restoration by physical restoration, so that when Rev. Moon passes there will be some families around through whom the Word is not only spiritually present, but continues to exist in some restored physical sense.

*Lloyd Eby:* I don't see those understandings as incompatible. I see them both as true. Rev. Moon's now about fifty-five, so how long can he live? Maybe twenty or thirty more years. Now, who knows how much will be accomplished within his lifetime? Clearly, many more things concerning the restoration of the world to God's Kingdom remain to be accomplished. I doubt that any other people now alive will have developed to the point where they have the ability to take over Rev. Moon's task.

*Linda Mitchell:* I would tend to disagree with that because in terms of the whole concept of sinless children, mankind will be able to develop a relationship with God and establish the Kingdom of Heaven. If what I'm saying is true, then Rev. Moon's children will inherit Rev. Moon's position and task. They are the beginning of that new tradition, as I see it. And they, as well as other families and other perfected children, are the continuation of that tradition.

*Dr. Kuykendall:* As you all see the eventuality and possibility, what would the relationship then be between the written words and the word as manifest in that generation of leadership? Will there be a shifting of relative authorities between the *Divine Principle* and a second generation of perfected leadership?

*Joe Stein:* It doesn't seem that there would be a great distinction between the word left behind and the word to be spoken. In other words, the developmental quality of our belief system is such that any new direction or new guides would grow out of the foundation of the past. So it doesn't seem to me that our future will be so different from what is already established.

*Klaus Lindner:* Rev. Moon doesn't add anything new on creation or fall or redemption or all those things. That's already laid down and hasn't changed since the book was written three years ago. He speaks about practical questions like what we're going to do this year, and about starting a Seminary and things like that.

*Dr. Clark:* One thing the Unification people have going for them that the early Christians didn't is that the question of whether or not the Kingdom comes in your theology depends on what you all do, whereas the early Christians were waiting for *God* to act to bring this Kingdom. And when it didn't occur, there was not only the problem of the delay of the *parousia* but the failure of the *parousia*. And what were the early Christians then to do with the God or the Messiah who did not bring what it was they thought He was supposed to bring? *You* can end up saying that you were to blame for the Kingdom's not coming because you didn't devote your whole hearts and minds and energies to this. I don't know if that would be better or worse. In any case, it will help in the preservation of the faith because you will feel more responsible for what happens.

*Dr. Wilson:* I'd like to shift the discussion. I can see some scientist saying, well, if the Unification perfect family is supposed to have perfect parents and perfect children, we will put on all the pressure we can to make sure that we find out whether the children are perfect or not. And if they aren't, then it would destroy the theory.

*Dr. Richardson:* Listen, I'm an imperfect parent, and I'd be willing to offer my own children up as a test of my imperfections. (laughter) I want to say that I don't think it's such a stupid notion. Just think about it on another level. A culture offers up its children as the mark of its integrity. You can speak of children rebelling and things like that, but it's not a problem if they go through a difficult three or four years in adolescence. Perfection is in the long run, and it seems to me that this is exactly what cultures offer. What you're trying to create here is a cradle for a new generation. All the patterns of child rearing and culture formation are finally vindicated in the crucible of the future generation, and if you don't bring forth a new generation that has new virtues, then your movement dies. One could talk about all the movements that died and became mere doctrine without any power whatsoever to affect a future generation. I think that your Unification vision is a very exciting vision.

*Jonathan Wells:* I'd like to second that and emphasize the element of practice and experimentation that comes in here. For example, it's not the case that Rev. Moon is a sharp fellow who has somehow convinced us that the principles are true, and we swallowed them intellectually and go along with him no matter what he does. It is the case that he has convinced us from our actual contact with him that he's working harder than any of us to be God's champion. In the course of that he has convinced us of the Principle. If leadership of the Church is transferred to his oldest son upon his death, and if his oldest son were to turn out somehow to be an ineffectual leader, then the Movement would die and the Principle would be proven false. On the other hand, if he turns out to be more energetic than we are, and a true champion of God, then the Principle is vindicated.

*Dr. Bryant:* Are you going to stick to the oldest son?

*Jonathan Wells:* Well, I don't know how it's going to happen. That's one possible scenario. But whoever takes the position is going to be able to hold the position only if that individual is the most energetic. This is the tradition that Rev. Moon has set up, and it's true of any leader in the Church.

*Guido Lombardi:* Rev. Moon himself has many times expressed a deep concern about the future and the element of chance in the coming of the Kingdom. He has spoken many times about tradition, and the importance of tradition, and his concern for the feeling that we have for tradition.

*Farley Jones:* I, too, would see that a logical succession would be down through the sons. I liked what Jonathan had to say too, but I might add that it very much depends on what those sons do. Just because they're born without sin doesn't mean they're perfect. They have to go through a period of proving themselves just as our original ancestors did.

*Dr. Bryant:* Let's go through this very slowly now. They are born without sin, yet they are not perfect. Right?

*Farley Jones:* Sinless children are born as the first ancestors were born, like a new family lineage that is born again. Children are being born without the spiritual death that our original ancestors incurred. But there's also that trial period. Every child, including Rev. Moon's children, has to go through a trial period where perfection depends very much on what they do. I think the fruit of Rev. Moon's work is very much to be seen in his family, although there are more immediate indicators than that. But the true indicator, the ultimate indicator of whether these things are working out properly, is if the truth or love of God can be incarnated and practiced: if these children can go through their period of testing, such as Adam and Eve did, and can reach the point where they can be totally trusted by God. Every family will eventually come to the point where there is no need of a mediator because there's a direct relationship with God. Every man will raise his family and grow up to the point where he, too, stands in the position of the Third Adam.

*Dr. Bryant:* Let me raise a question. Rod speaks of the family as a "highly disciplined and autocratically controlled community." I don't see that that's particularly bothersome to people. I would like to have some comments from people about how authority works within the family. I've been impressed with the initiative that comes from you people around various projects. The term "authoritarian" has certain negative connotations for me. But here it seems that authority is highly spiritualized. I'm just wondering if there should be any kind of qualification of those kinds of phrases. How does authority function in the community?

*Dr. Sawatsky:* Maybe we should specify a little bit. Who places whom in authority positions? I was asking Lloyd about who decides how this facility is going to be used; if buildings are going to be rebuilt, how are they going to be used? Who decides all the questions that any human community must deal with?

*Farley Jones:* These questions are decided by Rev. Moon. Questions about where to spend the money, and major undertakings like the rallies at Yankee Stadium and Washington Monument are all not only decided but often initiated by him.

*Dr. Sawatsky:* Who's going to be sent to the Chicago Center? Who decides that?

*Farley Jones:* Well, I think recommendations are made to Rev. Moon by people who know the personnel, and then he appoints someone.

*Linda Mitchell:* There's also a tremendous amount of initiation on our part. I think each one of us, because of the interest that we have, becomes involved, especially at the Seminary where we're in the kind of atmosphere that inspires creativity and new ideas. We get inspired by the thought of different kinds of projects and different things we want to see happen within the Church. We develop programs and present ideas which are, in many cases, adopted.

*Lloyd Eby:* I think that to answer this question you have to go back and pick up the notion of give-and-take, and the notion of family. We speak of ourselves as "The Family," and we think of ourselves, at least in a way, as Rev. Moon's children. And surely, it's the case in every family that when the children are young, their parents make almost all decisions for them. As they get older, the children make more and more decisions for themselves, and there comes a time when the parents are at the mercy of the children, more or less. I think, for example, of the Biblical account of Jacob sending his sons to Egypt during the famine. They came back and said that something had to be done and Jacob said he didn't agree, and they told him it had to be done anyway, regardless of his wishes. I think the same kind of dynamic is working here. The movement is young. As it ages, as more and more people come into the position where they become, as it were, "Rev. Moon's older children," he trusts them more and more and gives them more responsibility. He looks to them for inspiration, just as a parent looks to his children for inspiration.

*Joe Stein:* Another aspect is the fact that a tradition is being established at the same time. As the movement is growing it's developing a tradition of man's true individual relationship to God. Many people have the capacity to develop their concept of that tradition as it applies to the areas that they're most interested in, whether it be cultural or musical, or social or whatever. They can bring to Rev. Moon different ideas about what should be done.

*Jonathan Wells:* I'd like to say something actually agreeing with your statement here, Rod, but also in line with what Lloyd was saying about the general structure of the Church. And that is that for a new member, Unification usually, although not invariably, seems to be a very highly disciplined and autocratic organization. And quite commonly many of our Centers that are geared to receiving new members and training them spiritually are very highly disciplined. They have to be, as with any religious order. The training regime is quite carefully controlled and highly structured, although there's a lot of variation between Centers.

*Farley Jones:* I don't think Rod's is an unfair description.

*Lloyd Eby:* I react against it in a way, and yet I think it's a fair description. It's potentially misleading because, just as for many women the term "object" is very loaded, for many people the terms "authority" and "discipline" are very loaded kinds of concepts.

*Dr. Sawatsky:* I think what you're trying to say is that something ought to be said by way of suggesting that this is not to imply that the devotees are passive.

*Lloyd Eby:* Right. Also, in the times that I've heard Rev. Moon speak in the past year, I've noticed that he's talking much more about individuality and variations between people. My experience was that earlier he didn't stress that part and now he's stressing it a great deal. He's pointing out that each person is, in fact, an individual expression of God's nature. When he was here on Thursday he used this example. He said suppose one hundred of us here each eat a ham sandwich. What would our experience be? He pointed out that the experience of eating a ham sandwich would be different for each. The taste to me is not the same as the taste to you. I think he is pointing out that we can have an organization which has an essentially hierarchic form of discipline, but nevertheless, there is room for as much difference as there are different people. And that would imply as many different kinds of development.

*Dr. Richardson:* Could I take up something Lloyd just said that strikes me as a characteristic of the authority structure of the group, and that concerns the word "hierarchical?" I think the word "autocratic" is very tendentious and improper. I think the authority structure is something like this. In Western society, with its individualism, if you have a group, what you have is a bunch of individuals. And then if you have authority, you have one person over them. So one person is a boss over a lot of people and there are no mediators between the boss and the people. But in a feudal system or family system, the structure is hierarchical. Older brothers and sisters protect younger brothers and sisters from the parents. You have a feudal line of authority too. Everybody here in this room has spiritual children, and there's a sense in which those spiritual children are under your influence and authority even as you are under influence and authority. So there's practically nobody in this organization who isn't *in* authority, while also being *under* authority. This is one of the things that differentiates a hierarchial organization from, let's say, a democratic kind of authoritarian organization where either you're in authority or you're under authority. People tend not to experience organizations like this one as authoritarian because everybody experiences the person who is in authority over them as also under authority. Everybody is playing a double role.

*Dr. Sawatsky:* I wonder if that's so. Hierarchy is like a bureaucracy, and in a bureaucracy you report to the man above you, but you don't necessarily move all the way up. It seems to me that everybody here is directly connected to the man up top. Rev. Moon is over Toronto, Hong Kong, and every place, right down to localities here. This is not to say that there isn't another mediating structure as well, but I don't think we have here a thoroughly hierarchical structure.

*Dr. Richardson:* You're presupposing that hierarchic structures are bureaucratic, and I don't think they are. The ordinary kind of hierarchical structure is a family, and in a family everybody is older brother, middle brother, middle sister, and everybody knows where they belong hierarchically. The hierarchical structure in this kind of organic network of relationships seems to be different from a bureaucracy for a number of reasons. You say

Rev. Moon is over Toronto, Hong Kong and New York, and I don't think that's right.

*Dr. Sawatsky:* Okay, let's find out if that's right.

*Klaus Lindner:* In the European Church, many members have never even seen Rev. Moon. And in other countries they may never have seen him, and never have had a chance to talk to him. At the Seminary we are very close to where Rev. Moon lives. That's why we have a chance to talk to him and to see him. Yet the majority of the membership either has never seen him or has seen him once or twice as he spoke to a few thousand people. In the German Church, the leader of the German Church was a kind of a father figure for us, mediating Rev. Moon's presence.

*Lloyd Eby:* Something else needs to be said here, and that is that for most Americans the experience of authority has not been an especially good one. So the term authority has pejorative connotations. When Rev. Moon speaks about leadership, he speaks the same way as Jesus when Jesus said that whoever wants to be a leader is one who has to be the servant of all. In other words, that person is qualified to lead who shows excellence in empathy, in love, and in service.

*Dr. Wilson:* How do you know if somebody's loving more or serving more than others?

*Jonathan Wells:* It shows. If you're living with somebody day after day, you can tell who's working the hardest for the sake of everybody else.

*Dr. Wilson:* We need to ask what is the content of that service? I'm not sure that I can really find out what the content of service in the Unification Church is from the outside. Maybe selling more candy or whatever, but I don't know if I would necessarily conclude that that is an important service. What do you conceive of as criteria or standards for service?

*Jonathan Wells:* I think the standard that all of us look up to is the standard of Rev. Moon when he was in prison. There are many other instances, but this happens to be a particularly good story. And we don't just have this from Rev. Moon, but from other prisoners, too. When he was in prison under the Communists in North Korea, he couldn't teach verbally because he would have been executed. So he couldn't be a spiritual leader in that sense. What he did was, first of all, always take the most difficult job. He would work the longest hours, and would help the other prisoners. He divided his portion of food in half, and since the portion was only a fist-sized bowl of rice, that was quite a sacrifice. He'd give half of that to another prisoner. Half of them were starving anyway. And when his followers would bring him clothing and food from outside the camp, he invariably gave it away. It infuriated his followers, because they'd come back and see clothes they had brought him on some other prisoner's back. But in this way, he managed to attract a following in the camp. He became a very popular figure just by serving in this manner. That is a standard that he set for all of us.

The Unification ideal is that the individual should not live for himself, but live for his family, and the family for the Church, and the Church for the world. All the emphasis is on going beyond yourself.

# CRITICAL REFLECTIONS ON UNIFICATION ESCHATOLOGY

*M. Darrol Bryant*

At the outset I want to make a couple of things clear. This paper is not a finished statement. I rather understand it as a response to the conversations we had at the Unification Theological Seminary in the middle of February and to my admittedly limited reading of the *Divine Principle.* Its aim, therefore, is to further a dialogue already begun.

Eschatology within the Christian traditions has a checkered, diverse, underground, and ambiguous history. While Biblical scholars have recently reminded us of the centrality of the preaching of the Kingdom in the early Christian communities, the history of this notion within the Christian traditions is very uneven. In the credal affirmations of the faith, the matter is tersely stated: "I believe in . . . the Resurrection of the Body and the Life Everlasting" [Apostles' Creed], or "And I look for the Resurrection of the dead, and the Life of the World to come" [Nicene Creed]. Although such affirmations are common to most of the Christian traditions, the precise interpretation of these affirmations is diverse, even contradictory. These affirmations are understood in a variety of ways within the Christian traditions: they are sometimes spiritualized, while others give them an immanental or existential interpretation.

All bracketed references are to the *Divine Principle* (New York: The Holy Spirit Association for the Unification of World Christianity, 1973, 2nd ed.) unless otherwise noted.

Unlike Trinitarian and Christological doctrines, there are, to my knowledge, no "formulas" or "rules" that are widely considered normative in the development of eschatological doctrine. Yet throughout the history of the Christian traditions eschatology has had — and continues to have — a powerful, though unpredictable influence upon the theologies and practices of communities of faith. Many different movements and groups have emerged around a particular interpretation of the eschatological elements of Christian faith.

Hence I consider eschatological doctrine as the most fluid, open and indefinite aspect of Christian faith. We have few agreed-upon criteria for the evaluation or even consideration of theological proposals concerning the Last Things. In my judgment this is not accidental. Surely the "postponement of the *parousia*" had a profound impact upon the Christian community, so that the only affirmation that seemed possible was the general one indicated above: a statement of belief in the Resurrection of the Body and the Life of the World to come.

The matter is not quite so confusing if one asks how the Risen Christ is present to Christian communities and to the world. Here we can distinguish at least four traditions: (a) The Catholic tradition offers a sacramental answer: the Risen Christ is present in the sacraments, in His Body the Church, and in the World as a mystery; (b) The Reformed and Lutheran traditions believe that the Risen Christ is present in the preaching of the Word and in the world through our neighbor (Lutheran) or through the obedient exercise of our vocation (Calvinist); (c) The Anabaptist/Communalist tradition believes that the Risen Christ is present in the life of the separated community and not in "the world;" and (d) The Pietist/Personalist tradition believes that the Risen Christ is present in the hearts of believers and through them, in the world. However, these paradigms are not particularly helpful in relation to Unification eschatology which appears to return to a more "literal" belief in the Kingdom of God on earth. Moreover, it is not the question of the "Risen Lord *Jesus* Christ" which is at stake in Unification eschatology, but rather the question of the Messiah of the Second Coming who is not necessarily to be identified with the person of Jesus.

Thus it seems to me that Unification eschatology is in some respects dependent upon a new revelation, a "new truth" that is not to be found, at least explicitly, within the Christian traditions or in their normative sources. Yet at the same time, Unification eschatology does purport to fulfill and complete the belief in a Coming Kingdom which is found in Christianity.

These comments are not meant to be provocative, but simply to attempt to situate the question of eschatology within the Christian traditions and within Unification belief. Nor am I insisting that Unification eschatology cannot be considered a species of Christian eschatology — indeed Unification belief has many and obvious connections with millennial movements that have been a part of the Christian underground throughout history, and particularly millennial movements of nineteenth-century America. Furthermore, there is considerable evidence within the *Divine Principle* that its eschatology should be understood in Christian terms. I understand the *Divine Principle* to be offering an eschatology based partly on a reinterpretation of certain Biblical texts and ideas *and* partly on a new revelation. As it says in the *Divine Principle:*

> With the fullness of time, God has sent His messenger to resolve the fundamental questions of life and the universe. His name is Sun Myung Moon. . . . he came in contact with many saints in Paradise and with Jesus, and thus brought into light all the heavenly secrets through his communion with God. [16]

When one turns to the examination of the eschatology of the *Divine Principle* one must be aware of these two sources for its articulation. We shall return to this.

Unification eschatology is, as it should be, clearly linked to the doctrine of creation. Unification eschatology answers the question of *how:* how the process of restoration effects and completes the purposes of God intended in creation. This linkage of the doctrines of creation and consummation is characteristic of a fully articulated and internally consistent theological position. As such Unification eschatology satisfies two requirements of an adequate theological position: first, it satisfies the formal requirement of internal consistency and secondly, it provides the community of faith with an orientation which links their present activity in the world with the questions of ultimate origins and destiny.

There are three elements articulated in the Christian creeds which provide the starting point for a closer examination of the relationship of Unification eschatology to the Christian traditions. We have already mentioned "the resurrection of the body and the life of the world to come." I would also add the belief in Christ as the "one who shall come to judge the quick and the dead." In my judgment these three elements constitute the heart of the Christian faith concerning the Last Things. Taken together, they constitute a mystery: that is, Christians affirm "a judgment," a "resurrection of the body," and a "life to come," but they don't know how these beliefs are related, or precisely what they mean. As a "mystery" the question of the Last Things is open to a variety of interpretations and specifications. Indeed, one of the on-going tasks of theology is to meditate and reflect upon these beliefs so that our understanding may be deepened and our joy increased. Early on, most of the Christian tradition abandoned the attempt to impose a timetable on these beliefs or to specify a geography in which they would be realized. However, the "underground" of the Christian tradition did continue to offer very specific interpretations of these mysteries, complete with timetables, identification of the eschatological personages, and descriptions of the landscape of the coming Kingdom of God.[1] The *Divine Principle* is connected with that underground tradition.

No negative judgment is implied in relating Unification eschatology with so-called "underground" Christianity. Rather, it seems to me that Unification eschatology raises a number of important theological issues which the more mainline Christian traditions have either ignored or set aside. Unification eschatology challenges theology to think again about the questions of "the resurrection of the body" and "the life of the world to come," and thereby enters a sphere of much discussion in contemporary Christian theology.[2]

What, then, is Unification eschatology? As I indicated above, it is the completion and fulfillment of the doctrine of creation. Central to Unification eschatological doctrine are the paired notions of "The Second Advent of the Messiah" and "Resurrection." In the Unification theology these doctrines are the "engines" for the realization of the Kingdom of God on earth. Their connection with and divergence from the Christian traditions are important. Let us look at each of these notions separately.

The notion of the Second Advent of the Messiah is integral to Unification eschatology. The first advent of the Messiah was the coming of Jesus who effects "spiritual restoration." The full intention of God was the establishment of the Kingdom of Heaven on earth, but due to the non-acceptance of Jesus by the community of Israel, the mission was only half-successful. The Second Advent, therefore, completes this process of restoration by effecting a "physical restoration." The present age is understood as the "Last

---

[1]See for example, Norman Cohn, *Pursuit of the Millennium,* rev. ed., London: Paladin, 1970.

[2]Here I have in mind the contemporary discussion of eschatology associated with the theology of hope and liberation theology.

Days." According to Unification eschatology, we stand on the brink of a New Age, a time in which the Kingdom of God on earth can be achieved.

While Unification eschatology picks up themes central to the Biblical literature, it understands them in a novel way. If one takes for example the Book of Revelations on this question, then it is rather clear that the coming Lord who is anticipated there is the Lord *Jesus*. Rev. 22:20 says "Come Lord Jesus." Yet at the same time it must be acknowledged that the differentiation made in Unification thought between the Messianic office and the person of Jesus is not without precedent. Thus one can argue that the notion of the Second Advent is simultaneously continuous and discontinuous with a conventional understanding of the Second Advent in the Christian traditions. Moreover, it is important to distinguish Unification eschatology from the more fundamentalist eschatologies. Unification eschatology is not a literalist reading of the prophetic books of either the Old or New Testament. For example, the notion of the Last Days is not understood in an apocalyptic or literal-minded way, but rather in a cultural way. In the Last Days the previous ages of "formation" and "growth" are brought to "perfection." Hence Unification thought presents a view of the Last Days which denies neither the world nor history, but rather sees the world and history brought into a new configuration. The world and history are to be "God-centered."

Likewise, the Unification doctrine of the resurrection gives evidence of a complex and subtle theological principle at work. Resurrection, according to the *Divine Principle,* does not mean "the restoration of . . . once corrupted and decomposed physical bodies to their original state" [170] but rather "resurrection means to return to the Heavenly lineage through Christ, leaving the death of the Satanic lineage caused by the Fall of Adam." [171] This doctrine of resurrection is intimately related to the Unification notion of the Fall, a Fall which is transmitted "biologically." Thus Unification eschatology includes a solution to the problem of the Fall: a solution that adds to the "spiritual notion" of resurrection which is characteristic of the Christian traditions. That solution is, to me, highly ingenious and interesting: namely, a physical restoration which presumably will allow those so resurrected to produce sinless children.

Thus the notion of the Kingdom of God on earth is crucially linked to the mystery of the resurrection of the body. This resurrection is not postponed or supernaturalized, but is made a real possibility of these Last Days. Here, it seems to me, is an eschatology with a difference. One of the problems with other eschatologies that looked for the Kingdom of God on earth is this: where would the people come from who could populate a Kingdom of peace, unity, love, etc.? Without some mysterious transformation of man's bodily being, the hope for the transformation on the earth always seems to be exceedingly dubious. Unification eschatology, on the other hand, ties its belief in the Kingdom of God on earth to a notion of physical restoration, an interpretation of the doctrine of the resurrection of the body such that the attainment of "new bodily being" is coterminous with the idea of the Kingdom of God on earth. We read in the *Divine Principle* that

> The age in which the sinful world under Satanic sovereignty is transformed into the ideal world of creation under God's sovereignty is called the "Last Days" and means the age in which Hell on earth is transformed into the Kingdom of Heaven on earth. [111-112]

The Kingdom of Heaven on earth will not, however, be attained without conflict and struggle. The whole of human history is a prologue for the Last Days, yet each age has a distinctive role in preparing for these Last Days. For example, the "preparation period for the Second Advent of the Messiah is the four-hundred-year period from the Religious Reformation of 1517 to the end of World War I in 1918." [449] (This quotation is characteristic of the assurance with which the historical drama is interpreted in the *Divine Principle,* a self-assurance characteristic of eschatological literature in general. See for example Jonathan Edwards, *History of the Work of Redemption.*) This preparation period leads to our present situation of crisis. According to the *Divine Principle,* the upshot of this crisis is that

> the history of evil sovereignty centering on Satan will end with the appearance of the Lord of the Second Advent, and the history of evil sovereignty will be changed into the history of good sovereignty centered on God. Therefore, Satan at this time will put up his last struggle. [476]

It is difficult to know how to take some of these claims: symbolically, typologically, literally, historically, theologically? Nevertheless, it is clear that we find in the *Divine Principle* an astonishing specificity in its timetable for the eschaton. Such a tendency always threatens to turn eschatology — the theology of our destiny — into a blueprint for a proximate historical future.

In addition to this timetable of the Divine Economy, we find in the *Divine Principle* a clear identification of the major forces involved in this eschatological drama. The typology of the Cain-type or the "Satanic side" and the Abel-type or the "Heavenly side" is radically concretized and historicized. The forces of good and evil enter into a final and decisive conflict: the "Third World War." This war is inevitable although the mode of conflict — arms or ideologies — is not. Here the *Divine Principle* identifies, at one level, the "Satanic" and "Heavenly" forces with Communism and Democracy. However, it is during this period, our period, that there "must appear a new truth." [492] This "new truth" will be opposed to "dialectical materialism" [492] and

> when this new truth establishes a victorious basis in the democratic world and further subjugates the communist ideology, the one world under this one truth will finally be realized. [492]

The detail and concreteness of Unification eschatology at this point is astounding and is reminiscent of the apocalyptic visions that have characterized other movements and groups in the Christian traditions. The upshot of this conflict is that

> the victory of the Heavenly side in these three World Wars will finally enable the realization of the ideal world originally designed at the creation, which God has tried to fulfill through the long, long period of history since the fall of man, by completely restoring through indemnity all the foundations for the providence of restoration. [496]

It is in the midst of this period of conflict and victory that the Lord of the Second Advent appears. Indeed, the timing is insistent: "The Lord of the Second Advent must come between 1917 and 1930." [*Study Guide,* II, 119] The Lord of the Second Advent, according to the *Divine Principle,* will "be born on the earth as the King of Kings, and . . . will realize the Kingdom of God on earth." [509] As indicated earlier, the Lord of the Second Advent completes the restoration. He makes

> . . . the whole of mankind become one body with him by engrafting them to him both spiritually and physically, he must make them become perfect both spiritually and physically . . . [511]

The identity of this figure is not disclosed in the *Divine Principle,* although his continuity with the Christ is affirmed. According to the *Divine Principle,*

> Jesus by restoring the Kingdom of God on earth, should have become the True Parent of restored mankind and the King of the Kingdom on earth. Nevertheless, he failed to fulfill this will due to the

faithlessness of the people; he died on the cross, promising the Lord would come again later and surely fulfill it. Consequently, at the Second Advent, he must realize the Kingdom of God on earth as intended at Jesus' coming and become the True Parent of mankind and the King of the Kingdom as well. [511]

The temporal specificity of Unification eschatology is matched by its geographical specificity. The *Divine Principle* names Korea as the central location for the unfolding of the eschatological drama. This is argued typologically: Korea is understood to be the New Israel.

To my mind, this very specific geography and timetable raise major questions and criticisms. Surely the idea of Korea as the New Israel runs the danger of special pleading for the nation that gives rise to the Unification Movement. Moreover, the appeal of the Unification vision of the future becomes compromised by the very specificity of its eschatological timetable and landscape: is Unification eschatology vitiated if these details are incorrect? Furthermore, this excessive concretizing or immanentizing of the eschatological vision courts the twin dangers of literal-mindedness and fanaticism. If the Divine Economy is known with such detail, how is it possible to engage in dialogue with other communities? Why would one need to enter into discussion if the mind of God has been disclosed with such precision?

Yet — and this is the puzzle for me — these extremes do not characterize the Unification people that I have met. Earlier I indicated that eschatology has a twofold function: as part of a theological whole and as a way of orienting a community in time by relating the present to the questions of ultimate origins and destiny. On the second point — eschatology as the orientation of the community of faith in the present — I am impressed by what I have seen. The central image, unification, remains clear and unconfused by the details of this rather too specific eschatological landscape and timetable. Unification eschatology seems to have organized the energies of this community of faith as I have seen it in a commendable way. What I sense at the Unification Seminary is a community open to dialogue, a community with a sense of mission, direction and purpose but without fanaticism, a community in which the longed for consummation of the divine intention is anticipated in admirable forms of community life. However, the connection between what I see and much of what I read in the *Divine Principle* remains, for me, a puzzle.

In its articulated form, Unification eschatology is open to at least three kinds of criticism. First, is Unification eschatology an adequate reading of the Christian eschatological tradition? Although Unification is partly dependent on a "new revelation," it does claim to complete Christianity. Many, if not most, of its interpretations of the Biblical materials are open to question. And this is where the problem of the "new truth" comes in. Is there any way in which to resolve such disagreement between historical-critical interpretation of Scripture and Scripture read in the light of this "new revelation?" Moreover, Unification eschatology challenges the Christian communities to rethink the belief in the "Kingdom of God on earth." What does Unification theology mean by the "Kingdom of God on earth?" Is it a visible Kingdom?

Second, is Unification eschatology essentially Manichean? That is to say, does not Unification eschatology end in an unwarranted, or at least questionable, identification of the forces of good with democracy and the forces of evil with Communism? It is this aspect of Unification eschatology which I find most suspect. The reasons for that suspicion involve a judgment about the fundamental ambiguity of all historical phenomena, so that one must always temper one's reading of historical forces with a strong dose of self-criticism. I am not saying that we make no attempt to "read the times," but rather that any reading of the times must acknowledge that the final differentiation of the meaning of historical events is a divine, not human, prerogative, even if the human differentiation claims to rest on divine revelation.

The third level of criticism involves the relationship of typology and history. Can one move from typological constructs, e.g., Cain-type and Abel-type, to specific historical movements? I find such moves laden with difficulties. How, for example, can such ideal-types be adequately related to the real-types of history? Does not the Cain-Abel typology point to a fundamental conflict that runs *through* every historical person, institution or movement rather than *between* historical persons, institutions and events?

These criticisms return us to the three elements that characterize Christian eschatology, at least in the Creeds, namely, the world to come, the resurrection of the body, and the Last Judgment. Unification eschatology omits any discussion of the Last Judgment. It appears that the Last Judgment has been immanentized and historicized. Hence, the Judgment is not left as a divine prerogative at the end of time, but is taken into time as the prerogative of those who know the Divine Will in detail. This is, I believe, a dangerous mistake. Yet at the same time, Unification eschatology offers an interpretation of the "resurrection of the body" and the "world to come" which I find both challenging and worthy of consideration.

Finally, I believe that the eschatology found in the *Divine Principle* needs to be developed in a more careful way. For example, the last entry in the *Divine Principle* concerns the "One World and One Language." I find this to contain an instructive confusion, namely, the tendency to identify the One World which is longed for with a world in which everyone speaks *the same language*. The Unification notion of unification is much richer than that and needs to be articulated in a way which will overcome this confusion. The meaning of "unification" as it is exhibited in this community is much closer to the Pentecost experience: all spoke in their own tongues and were understood by each other. Isn't that the eschatological end we seek?

## DISCUSSION IV

*Dr. Clark:* I think your point about the omission of any discussion of the Last Judgment is very interesting and well taken, and I would like to hear the Unification response.

*Jonathan Wells:* Well, I'll tell you this: every Sunday morning at five o'clock, we get up and have a service, where we pledge our lives to God, and in our pledge, we talk about judgment.

*Dr. Bryant:* Is that a kind of credal statement? Something you repeat every Sunday morning?

*Jonathan Wells:* Right. The whole spirit of it is that we reaffirm our commitment to creating the ideal world and the ideal family, and the Last Judgment is cast in these terms: "I will follow our Father's pattern and charge (this is pretty militant) bravely forward into the enemy camp until I have judged them completely with the weapons with which he has been defeating the enemy Satan for me throughout the course of history by (now, here's the judgment) sowing sweat for earth, tears for man, and blood for heaven (my blood) as a servant, but with a father's heart, in order to restore God's children and the universe." This is the key, I think, to the Unification attitude, "sowing sweat for earth, tears for man, and blood for heaven, as a servant, but with a Father's heart." That's the judgment. By that standard, the world is judged.

*Dr. Bryant:* Well, I think that's pretty much my point, especially as you read the first sentence: that you extend the Father's judgment in the world.

*Dr. Sawatsky:* Is that an interpretation of what you find in the New Testament, namely, that Christ's presence is already the judgment? That's what I take your creed to be saying: the possibility of new life is automatically expessed in the judgment on the state of affairs as they are.

*Jonathan Wells:* It's self-judgment, really. It seems to be characteristic of Unification theology that you don't end up at a point where some group or other of the human race is unredeemable. I think Unification theology would want to say that there is a way that everyone can be saved.

*Dr. Sawatsky:* Is Unification universalist?

*Tom Selover:* I think that's right. There's not a sense that some make it, others don't and that's it.

*Dr. Sawatsky:* Right, but there's no prescription as to how this takes place for those who've already died.

*Dr. Bryant:* I would like to get the story straight here. Is there a doctrine of universal salvation?

*Farley Jones:* We don't envision an eternal damnation, but we envision that all mankind will ultimately be restored. For some this won't happen till after they've entered the spirit world, but growth is possible in the spirit world.

*Dr. Bryant:* Why, then, would you be so concerned about the Communists or any other group that would seem to be opposed to you? Isn't it just a matter of time for them to be restored?

*Joe Stein:* The physical earth, for us, is the sphere of the greatest opportunity for growth. The physical world is the world in which we can fulfill the blessings. So in order to enter into the spiritual world having accomplished the three blessings, we have to realize those three blessings during our physical life on earth. Therefore, the maintenance of religious freedom on the earth in order to allow individuals to develop their relationship with God must be protected within the earthly sphere. So even the concept of resurrection that we have is a concept of resurrection of individuals within the spiritual world, the restoration of their relationship to God within the spiritual world through counterparts, and through their cooperative ministry with individuals who are living on earth. So in this context, to maintain spirituality on earth is very important. Hence a doctrine that is materialistic or atheistic would make it far more difficult for individuals to grow spiritually. This would prolong the restoration process; it would make it more complicated for God to be able to work to restore His Kingdom on earth. So a doctrine such as Communism or an ideology with a materialistic base would create greater difficulties for the establishment of the Kingdom of God on earth; even though, in time, all things will be restored.

*Linda Mitchell:* I think there's also a very real belief that we can establish God's Kingdom on earth. Until that Kingdom is established, more and more people will die, and more and more people will suffer, so this is the time when, in fact, God's ultimate ideal can be fulfilled. It is a consequence of our desire to serve other people, to serve all mankind that leads us to want to alleviate that suffering at the earliest possible moment.

*Joe Stein:* What Linda says is very important. Not only is the suffering of man prolonged, but also the suffering of God. So it's God's longing and man's longing at the same time to see the establishment of God's Kingdom on earth.

*Dr. Bryant:* I understand that. The point is your assurance in executing God's judgment on earth. You claim to know God's longing and will very precisely about this group or that group, this movement or that movement.

*Dr. Sawatsky:* I think that's too harsh. In the New Testament the whole discussion of the Advocate is that he will convict or convince the world of sin, judgment and righteousness. That's linked with the activity of his disciples. In fact it is through the activity of the new Israel that that self-judgment of the world is made. Unification's notion of judgment seems to be consistent with that.

*Linda Mitchell:* I think it is very important to make a distinction here. In the Christian tradition when you're talking about judgment it's related to the question of eternal damnation. But we're talking about the portion of good and evil in the world, we're talking about something that we're working not to destroy, but to change to the side of good. So when Jesus, for example, is damning the Scribes and the Pharisees, and telling them exactly where they stood in terms of a heavenly standard, he didn't mince any words at all. Jesus didn't say, okay, you're going to Hell now, and this is your judgment, but he was setting forth the standard so that they could see where they stood, so that they could change. I think that our judgment of Communism and the way we feel God is working is for that purpose, not for eternal judgment. Hence you can't compare the Last Judgment that you're talking about with our view of Communism or good and evil in the world.

*Dr. Bryant:* What I'm saying is that, first of all, within the *Divine Principle,* there is no discussion of the Last Judgment, which would be one of the things that one would expect to see within an eschatology. I'm saying it's not there. I am wondering where this doctrine goes within Unification eschatology? Secondly, it strikes me that one reason that it's not there formally or explicitly is because it gets incorporated into the historical timetable and geography of Unification eschatology as a way of discriminating what is going on in this world at the present time or in these last days. Hence, there's no longer any tension between the present historical situation and an ultimate situation. This, it seems to me, is the point of the Last Judgment within the Christian tradition. Now, that doesn't mean that within the Christian tradition there are not all kinds of judgments of particular groups and movements. Catholics, Lutherans, Dutch Reformed, they all know who the good guys and the bad guys are in terms of the practice of particular communities. But the point is that theologically there's a good reason for not grounding such judgments in the Divine will. And that reason is that you understand that judgment is finally a divine prerogative. It stands at the end of time. We make relative judgments but not ultimate judgments. In the eschatology of the *Divine Principle,* the doctrine of the Last Judgment isn't there, and it's not there, I suspect, because it's brought into a time in history, our time.

*Farley Jones:* Our definition of judgment is separation of good from evil. I think we see it as a process that goes on within the individual, in the family, in the nation and in the world, step by step, resulting in the transformation of evil into good. I think that's how we envision it. The ultimate, final goal is, according to our understanding, a final realization of a good world, the Kingdom of God on earth, and elimination of evil.

*Dr. Richardson:* I'd like to make two points. The first is, contra Darrol, a kind of a systematic point. If you have a post-millennialist eschatology, by which we mean in traditional Christianity, Jesus comes back after the millennium is established, then we usually do not have a doctrine of the Last Judgment. In post-millennialist eschatologies you don't have a separation of good from evil, you have a victory of good over evil, and the establishment of the Kingdom, so that the historical function of the Last Judgment isn't there. Then the question is, well, what about the people who died before the millennium was established? One has, I think, in Unification theology a very reasonable point, namely, that the people who died before the millennium continue to grow through the continual activity of righteous people. Once you have established the millennium on earth, you'll get righteous action, which will lead to the growth of people in heaven, and so you don't even need a final judgment in that way. Secondly, I would argue that it's a very perceptive, very interesting systematic point, that what happens to the Last Judgment, in a post-millennialist theology, is that it is lost because the function of judgment in a sense belongs to the millennial activity of the Christian community.

I'd like to move the discussion to another area, namely, the matter of historic specificity. I think it's perfectly clear that the longer Christian tradition tended to argue partly on the Augustinian line of no separation of the sheep and goats until the Last Judgment and partly on the basis of a notion of the church as a spiritual organism that can live in any political climate at all. The assumption was that all times and places are pretty much the same. But I think we should relook at this matter. Let me give an example. Last summer I was riding in Europe, going up the road with French signs and suddenly I realized the signs were German. We stopped at the next town, and I walked in and I said, "How come they speak French five miles away and here they speak German?" And the answer of the woman in the drugstore was, "Well in 1368, there was a great battle just outside the town. The French were invading, but we won. That's why everyone here speaks German, and over there they speak French." And if you drive up the road another 100 miles you see the remains of the Roman settlement across Northern Europe, where the Roman walls were, where defensive lines were, and what essentially that meant was that there, behind the Roman walls, you had the development of cities, a degree of cosmopolitanism. You simply had no civilization south of that wall. Now, there are some significant points here. There is a geopolitical or a political dimension to human history. Historically you've only been able to have certain teachings and the Christian Church in certain geographical settings. It was the Roman Empire that made possible the Christian Church. I think we could even say that it is not the case that ideas float freely around the world in the free market of ideas. There are political realms in which the circulation of certain ideas is a possibility, and the other places where that is not possible. It strikes me that there are, in history, and we know this, decisive times, and there are decisive spaces. It seems to me merely consequential that any church that believes that the Kingdom of God is going to be established on earth is going to fight for the importance of that idea in general. Maybe we're not going to agree that this decisive battle line is Korea, but, the general idea of special spaces is, it seems to me, defensible. I think similarly about the question of decisive time. I find it difficult to think that we can't believe that we are in a very decisive period of history. When you think in social, rather than individualistic terms, then of course you have decisive times and spaces.

*Dr. Bryant:* Right. I agree about that. You noticed, didn't you, that I didn't make any criticism of the notion of the "Last Days?" I even said that they have a pretty good understanding of the Last Days as opposed to the fundamentalists. But I still find the specificity of the eschatology disturbing. For example, statements like the Lord of the Second Advent must be born between 1917 and 1930. I don't think that any faith wants to be tied that specifically to any predictions. Another problem is that there's a failure to make a distinction between prophecy and prediction. In a sense Unification eschatology falls into the trap of modern-day social science: confusing prophecy with predictions of the future. That's not good prophecy.

*Mike Jenkins:* I think our view of history is very flexible, extremely flexible. Yet, there's a tendency when examining history in the *Divine Principle* that we want to change a lot of details, to flush out a lot of for instances and examples. But in doing so, you risk losing the point of the whole history. The point of the presentation is to shed light on the possibility that we are living in the time of the Second Advent. That's the whole point of the history. It's not to show that this is all factual, but that there's a general system of parallels or cyclical development, that God's plan is working from the very beginning of the first ancestors to now. In relation to the idea that the Lord of the Second Advent is born between 1917 and 1930, I believe that's true. I believe the *Divine Principle* is true. But I don't go around saying that this is the only truth. We're presenting this as a possibility. But it remains to be seen whether it's true for other people.

*Jonathan Wells:* Exactly, I would say that it's actually an advantage to all of us to have this precise chronology. It makes the whole thing very concrete. If it isn't true, then we don't have to wait around for three or four hundred years. (laughter) We'll know in our lifetime.

*Dr. Bryant:* I've heard, from others, that "normal eyes" would not be able to see the Kingdom on earth. It seemed that you'd at least have to have the spiritual eyes to see this Kingdom, even when we're living right in the middle of it. I think there's disagreement within the Unification Movement on this point.

*Jonathan Wells:* I'm sure you'll find differences. But I think there is a lot of specificity in what Rev. Moon himself predicts. I know that when Rev. Moon came five years ago, the movement here was very small, and yet he came and said, "Well, in a couple of years, my name will be a household word all over the United States." (laughter) Most people didn't believe him, and yet, it was true. He constantly does this.

*Tom Selover:* Yes, but when Rev. Moon points the movement

in a particular direction then we unite and go out and do it. The timetable is a possibility, it doesn't unfold mechanically.

*Mike Jenkins:* We can maybe firmly believe that the Messiah will come between 1917 and 1930, but everything after that depends upon the response of the people.

*Linda Mitchell:* We believe that it is the case that the Lord of the Second Advent was born between 1917 and 1930. But I think that the *Divine Principle,* at least as I understand it, is trying to say that we have these historical parallels which allow us to understand how God has been working through history. Given these parallels we can see that it would make sense that the Messiah must come between 1917 and 1930. I think it's important to have this understanding of what we're saying. We're saying that because history has followed this and this course, then we can have this expectation.

*Dr. Bryant:* But is it history that's followed this pattern? Isn't it the typology that's developed in the *Divine Principle* that has this pattern? There's a distinction between typology and history. When I read about the period from 1517 to 1918 as a period of preparation, I see it as a device, a typology and not a description of history. On a straight historical plane, we'd have to allow all kinds of qualifications. A typology operates on a different basis.

*Dr. Richardson:* Aren't you being overly dense? Why the years 1917 to 1930? It's perfectly obvious why. It isn't that Rev. Moon is born in 1920. The explanation is something like this. Given the importance of the year 2000 and realizing that the year 2000 figures from the birth of Jesus, and realizing that there is this three-year discrepancy about the date Jesus is born, then you need a beginning date that fits. You're working very seriously from the figures of Jesus and you understand that the year 2000 has a significance. Now, then, you have the notion of a Messiahship, where there's going to be a central figure who, over the course of a whole life, is going to do a perfect work, and over the course of a whole life, he has to live a life of three score years and ten, a scriptural age. So this central figure has to be at least seventy in the year 2000 or in his seventieth decade. Now, what is the importance of 1930: a man born in 1930 would be at least seventy years old, he'd have to be at least seventy in the year 2000, and he could be no more than eighty, so that's the reason for 1920, and you pick up the other three years because of the uncertainty about Jesus' birth and so you've got 1917 to 1930. Admittedly this is a complex thing. There is much more involved than just picking a date out of the air. You've got the belief in historical cycles, the importance of the year 1000, the notion of the Messiahship, something more than just numerology. Just on the practical level, we know the year 2000 is going to be a critical year. I mean, the year 1000 was, and they didn't have mass media in those days. (laughter) I mean, the year 2000 is going to be a time of cataclysmic historical crises. The messianic and apocalyptic speculation is going to go wild. There's a sense in which one is playing with myth here. And this is the hottest myth in the next twenty years, and if any one of us were developing a preaching program for one of the traditional denominations, we'd want to build it around the year 2000. And then, when you put this in relation to the energy crisis, expanding Marxism, the ecological crisis and so forth and so on, and you begin to speculate about historical, political circumstances in that framework, I think you've got the elements for a great drama. (laughter)

*Dr. Bryant:* Well, I agree on that level. But the *Divine Principle* is not simply playing with eschatological myths. These people believe it! (laughter).

# BIOGRAPHICAL SKETCHES OF
# UNIFICATION CHURCH PARTICIPANTS

*Janine Anderson,* 24, studied philosophy at Reed College in Oregon. She has lived in Italy for several years and speaks Russian, French, and Spanish in addition to Italian. She joined the Unification Church three years ago and is a member of the class of 1978 at the Unification Theological Seminary.

*Christa Dabeck,* 25, is from Germany, where she met the Unification Church five years ago. She did her undergraduate work at the University of Regensburg where she studied history, sociology, and German literature. She is a member of the class of 1978 at the Unification Theological Seminary.

*Adri de Groot,* 27, graduated from the Unification Theological Seminary in 1977 and is currently in a Master of Divinity program at Boston University. His intent is ultimately to obtain his doctorate. He is a native of Holland, where he met the Unification Church five years ago.

*Lloyd Eby,* 34, has been a member of the Unification Church for four years. Already the possessor of a Master's degree in philosophy from Washington University in St. Louis, he graduated from the Unification Theological Seminary in 1977 and is currently considering pursuing his doctorate. In addition to philosophy and theology, Lloyd has studied film making and is the producer/director of a short film about the Unification Theological Seminary.

*David Jarvis,* 30 years old, a 1977 graduate of the Unification Theological Seminary, is the possessor of two B.A. degrees and is currently doing graduate work at the Divinity School of the University of Chicago. He has been a Unification Church member almost three years.

*Michael Jenkins,* 25, received his B.S. in zoology from Ohio State University. He has been a member of the Unification Church for four years and graduated from the Unification Theological Seminary in 1977.

*Betsy Jones,* 34, did undergraduate work in nursing at Boston College and received a Master's in psychiatric nursing through Columbia Teachers College. She is married to Farley Jones and is the mother of three children.

*Farley Jones,* 34, received his B.A. in English from Princeton University. He has been a Church member for eleven years and will graduate in 1978 from the Unification Theological Seminary.

*Lynn Kim,* 29, is a ten-year member of the Unification Church. She graduated from Lawrence University in Wisconsin in foreign languages.

*Klaus Lindner,* 25, graduated from the Unification Theological Seminary in 1977 and is currently enrolled in a Master's of Theology program at Harvard Divinity School, where he would like to pursue doctoral studies. He met the Unification Church five years ago in his native Germany.

*Guido Lombardi,* 27, has been a member of the Unification Church for five years. He is an Italian citizen and did undergraduate work in sciences at the University of Rome. He was a member of the class of 1977 at the Unification Theological Seminary.

*Lokesh Mazumdar,* born in India, graduated from Montana State University with a B.S. in commerce. He is 32 years old and for six years has been a member of the Unification Church. He belonged to the class of 1977 at the Unification Theological Seminary.

*Linda Mitchell,* 25, for three years a member of the Unification Church, studied Italian and Portuguese at California State University. She is a member of the class of 1978 at the Unification Theological Seminary.

*Diana Muxworthy,* 26, joined the Unification Church three years ago. She graduated from the University of New Hampshire in social sciences. Diana belonged to the class of 1977 at the Unification Theological Seminary.

*Thomas Selover,* 26, has been a member of the Unification Church for three years. He graduated from Virginia Wesleyan College with a B.A. in education and was a teacher in the Waldorf school program. A member of the class of 1977 at the Unification Theological Seminary, Tom is presently considering obtaining his doctorate.

*Tirza Shilgi,* 31, was born in Israel and met the Unification Church four years ago in America. She graduated from the Becalel Academy of Fine Arts where she did work in sculpturing, woodcutting, and silkscreen. She is in the class of 1978 at the Unification Theological Seminary.

*Joe Stein,* age 28, has been a member of the Unification Church since 1969. He did undergraduate work in psychology at the University of Rochester and intends to pursue doctoral studies. He is a member of the class of 1978 at the Unification Theological Seminary.

*Joe Stenson,* age 27, has been a member of the Unification Church for three years. He graduated from the Catholic University of America and belonged to the class of 1977 at the Unification Theological Seminary.

*Jonathan Wells,* 35, has been a Church member for three and one half years. He earned an A.B. in physical science from the University of California at Berkeley. He is in the class of 1978 at the Unification Theological Seminary and he plans to study for a doctorate.

The Unification Theological Seminary was founded in 1975 in Barrytown, New York. It occupies 250 acres of land next to the Hudson River, ninety miles north of New York City. The Seminary has applied to the New York State Board of Regents for a charter to grant Master's degrees in religious education, and more than one hundred men and women are presently enrolled in a two-year program in religious education.

The purpose of the Seminary is to promote interfaith, interracial, and international unity. This purpose is reflected in the unique composition of its faculty, which includes representatives from the major branches of the Jewish and Christian traditions, for example, Roman Catholicism, Greek Orthodoxy, Reformed Protestantism, Free Church, and Rabbinic Judaism. The academic program provides broad-based preparation in Biblical studies, church history, theology, philosophy, and psychology. Graduates are expected to assume Church or civic leadership positions, and to promote unity between Christian denominations and other religions. In addition to the regular course of study, students frequently participate in conferences with visiting theologians, such as the one recorded in this book.